A Beach in Portu;

And at that very moment
All the reasons why I love you flash before my eyes
In one inconceivable word
A thought of such knowing
A feeling that a single expression could not touch or
comprehend.

I have had the body of Christ wiped across my tongue
I knelt before my god, to give thanks for my life
I would not live, for my heart could not give

But now my sight is changed
My mind is reborn
The sun shines even when it hides its face
The winds of confidence bought me to your shores

Those rainy days of no consequence
Are now brimming with droplets of hope
And the snow, oh the snow
It covers all in a blanket of beauty
Is all this what I saw? What I felt

That split second that instance now gone
But held forever in my blushing heart
These thoughts we cannot grasp but know are right

As Steve Hogarth once said it all started with the bright light and the noise. And so it was for Tracey and I, that circumstance, pure chance or fate conspired in their separate ways to ensure we met. I know you may say it is just happy remembering, but when I first saw her pass me by I knew I would marry her, keep her and hold her forever (gospel I did).

Gospel was always something we would say to each other to underpin a true thought or feeling. It is weird really that a religious word could give such levity for us, used in a statement of love, reassurance or just to boost each other's confidence. Because by the time you close this book a belief in all heavenly angels has truly been shattered for both of us.

So we courted and we married, we bought houses and cars. We smoked, we drank, we laughed, and yes, we argued, but deep down in both our hearts we knew this was bliss. We held something very precious that could not be put into words. It was just a deep knowing on both sides that in some way, we were blessed.

And so it was that the snowflakes drifted amongst the night sky like falling stars, as I stood holding Tracey's hand as she gave birth to our daughter, our delicious almost edible child, all rosy cheeks and blonde locks, and Tracey's inherited determination as she grew. Three years gently passed, with each day weighed down, tied to the reality of a young family. A house that needed work and a desire to embrace the growing circle of family and friends that were around us.

THE DEATH
OF A COMMON MAN'S WIFE

FOR TRACEY
12/11/1962 to 8/8/2014

Our return to Good Hope Hospital on the 12th August 1993, unlike our recent future visits, yielded another positive outcome. He was late, but as we look at him today he is relaxed, he sits comfortably in our worlds. Again, I held my wife's hand as she bore him to this world and I cut the cord that would release him from her care. It was magical. We are now complete, happy and content.

But as we know so well Tracey never let the dust settle for too long. The detritus of this world never lingered long beneath her feet - she would kick it away, 'that was a beautiful day, but what about tomorrow?'

'Tomorrow', I would say, 'is just another day'. But to Tracey it was a fresh new dawn. A dawn that we all have seen. That gentle frost upon our lawns, crisp and white, her twisting footprints, the first to pierce the freezing blanket that stretched before her eyes, making her mark, barefoot abandonment, and cold realisation that you are your heaven and you can be your own hell if you want it. But we all reap what we sow.

So by 1998 it was time to go, to turn another page of her life that enveloped my own, that pushed me to be a better man. She always knew what she wanted, and although I sometimes wallowed in self-doubt with chips on each shoulder, she wanted me, she needed me, and for that alone I loved her deeply. She saved me.

Mr McIntosh had lived at Redacre Road for some 30 years. He and his late wife had cherished every room - you could feel the scent of family life escape from each corner and curve. It took but a moment for us to love this house and in some ways love this man who was passing it over to us, placing it in our care to regenerate its laughter within another generation. April 1st saw eight new footprints run across its lawns, bound up its stairs, relax in its rooms and sleep within its dreams. The memories that stir mixed with the new, silent and unseen since 1927. How many families and how many friends have turned each glass door knob throughout this home? And now, how many are to follow us on? Well, many came for us with goodwill and shining hearts, so much joy within four walls, from Christmas tide to the returning fall of autumn leaves. You have to admit it was fun.

Sometimes when you meet someone you just get sex, sometimes you get heat, lust then sex. For the lost you get lust, sex and entrapment. But occasionally you can get all of the above, with a joyous entrapment, coupled with a complete respectful love. And this is how it was for us, even when I placed my clothes neatly on the beach of life and swam out to sea with all the angst of Reginald Perrin piercing my mind, pulling at my ankles. She stood there petrified but still she supported me, and in all fairness, I repaid the faith she had in me 10 fold, because from 2010 to the date she left us, I earned more money.

we travelled the world, we schemed and we planned, I embraced her world because my mind was finally free. If you can picture a tethered deer breaking loose from its captor, sit back in wonder as it skips and almost dances on the air into freedom, into the woods to find its family, never to look back. Never ever to look back. She, this wonderment of womanhood gave me that chance, that fleeting skip over woodland heather, over burning bracken over all my previous fears, into all that lay before us.

So my tale that had only really just started, is sadly coming to its end. Because on Monday 30th December 2013, the dimming of the brightest light began.

Monday 30th December 2013

The alarm went off as usual at 6.00am, and it was as I started to get ready that I got really chronic low down tummy pain, almost like labour pains. I rang work to say that I would be late, but after taking some tablets, the pain subsided. I drove to work and the pain was okay for the rest of the day. I decided to re-book the Doctor's appointment that I had cancelled at the end of last year (I had training!) Now booked in for 8th January.

Monday 6th January 2014

I woke up again with tummy pain, which was worse when standing. Fortunately, I got an appointment with Dr Clarke, who is a senior lady Doctor. After examination she was happy to refer me on, a two week wait. As previous blood results suggested I was post-menopausal she said she couldn't feel anything sinister, but this is the quickest way to be seen and that the hospital would do all necessary checks. I went into work.

7th & 8th January 2014

My tummy kept on grumbling like it was second or third day period pain. I was concerned about my holiday insurance for Krakow, that if I would be taken ill whilst away, as I hadn't even booked it yet.

Thursday 9th January 2014

Simon's Christmas present. We flew to Poland and arrived early evening. It was a great, hotel like an up-market Travel lodge. We had lots to drink, a lovely meal and great conversation. We tried a traditional Polish meal and drank Polish vodka. A great start to the holiday.

10th, 11th & 12th January 2014

POLAND. Loved it! I even preferred it to Prague, although I felt that Simon was a little apprehensive. We went to Schindler's factory, which was really interesting, although the area was pretty bleak. Then we met some lovely people and set off to the salt mines. What a great afternoon! Fantastic company, especially considering I never normally make friends on holiday. But, the two couples were great fun - the one northern girl was a scream while we trolled around the salt mines on a three hour tour. The next day we went to Auschwitz, which was fascinating although a little depressing. It is not the sort of place for laughs or great conversation, but I'm so pleased I've actually been. I'm glad we watched Schindler's List before the visit as it really bought it all to life.

Wednesday 29th January 2014

Today I had an appointment to see Dr Cartmell at Good Hope Hospital. I knew there was a problem following the call from a nurse the previous day, asking me to bring someone with me. A nurse called Vanessa was is the room as Dr Cartmell delivered shocking news that a biopsy had found cancerous cells, though apparently "sleepy cancer cells", at Stage 1, Grade 1A/1B.

Terribly upset but was told that a hysterectomy was curative, and that if there was a cancer to have, this was the one! Rang work and said I would be off until Monday.

The unknown is always there to trap us
To feed us a lie of relief
Are we able to fold our fingers, bend our belief
To beat this lie of life
Hold an outstretched hand to the dark
Of yet unknown grief

For the first time on a long road I am fearful of what lies ahead
I look at former cloudless skies, with overwhelming dread
Suffocated by memories of the former dead

Friday 31st January 2014

Today was my MRI scan, which was quite scary, but I kept my eyes tightly shut throughout. It was very noisy and seemed to take ages, but nurses were lovely and I got through it. Went to Debbie's in the evening, I felt lovely, wore skinny jeans, heels and a stripy top. Felt slim and amazing, and up for a drink.

Deb had got her results, and all was okay but she knew something was up with mine. I told the girls towards the end of the evening and they were lovely, felt so positive and, strangely, I was on a real high.

Saturday 1st February 2014

Went to Britain's got Talent with Angela and Matt. We had a brilliant time, it was so much fun. Got train back to Boldmere then had a fab curry at Shaban. I wasn't sure whether to tell them, but decided to at the end of the evening. Obviously they were quite upset, poor Matt didn't feel too well. We had all got soaked in town then drank quickly and eaten in a hot restaurant. I think he was a bit overcome and he started to faint. After reviving him, we went our separate ways and everything glossed over, which suited us.

3rd - 11th February 2014

I had told work about the outcome as I was supposed to attend an important meeting after having the results. I told Debbie, the Practice Manager at Ley Hill Surgery, who let the girls know how I had got on.

I carried on going to work and the first week was okay, although I felt that the girls were tip-toeing around me a bit. But, if I was up, they tried their best to keep me cheery.

Unfortunately I didn't hear anything before the weekend and to my distress there was no news on Monday or Tuesday again. I felt tense.

Dr Beaumont called me in to her room and rang Mr Cartmell's secretary to try and speed up the appointment, but there was still no news.

I came home and lay on the settee. Felt like shit. Was supposed to go to Sue's for tea at 4.30pm but could not get off the sofa. I was hoping to receive a phone call following MDT meeting to get a date to see the consultant. Jon gave me one of his inspirational talks and told me to just go to Sue's - that it would cheer me up. I'm so glad I did, I arrived a bit late, but had a great time with the girls. They are the bestest friends.

Wednesday 12th February 2014

Vanessa, the Macmillan Nurse from Good Hope, called to get me in the next day for an appointment with Mr Bolega, in the Sheldon block at Good Hope. Thank goodness.

Thursday 13th February 2014

Waited ages in the Sheldon unit. What a depressing place. There are cancer leaflets everywhere, old poorly people, a wig department and even photos of ways to wear head scarves!

But what a lovely man Mr Bolega is. He's quite young, handsome and obviously brilliant. He makes eye contact with you and makes you believe every word he says. He explained the operation and answered all of our questions. Afterwards we sat with a lovely blonde young Macmillan nurse who answered more questions, and drew us a clearer picture, which put our minds at rest. Just got to wait for the date now...

Saturday 22nd February 2014

Fabulous evening with Sue, Steve, Mandy and Richard at Kababish. It wasn't too expensive really, and I couldn't believe how well the six of us gelled; probably even better than when it was eight of us.

Sunday 23rd February 2014

I went to Birmingham with Simon to try and find an outfit for Sarah's 50th. It was a rubbish day; I felt weepy and miserable for the entire day and couldn't find a thing to wear. Simon found a few clothes with his birthday money. I will probably just wear something I've already got in my wardrobe.

Bloody pen has run out!!! I hate blue!!!

Monday 24th February 2014

After work I took myself off to T.K.maxx, which is my favourite shop, and bought four dresses, a handbag and some figure shaping tights, then went home. God, how good shopping is, I got a real buzz from it. I do like shopping after all - it just has to be the right shop.

Tuesday 25th February 2014

My pre–op was booked for 11am at City Hospital, Simon took half a day off and we went over, had a lovely Costa coffee in the hospital Cafe as it was soooo early. Then we saw some nurses who did height, weight, bp history etc. They were all so good and in and out within a couple of hours. Booked myself in for a massage to ease my aching back and shoulders.

Lee (Lisa) had given me her number some time ago, but I felt the time was right now as my shoulders and neck were so tense. Bloody hell, she hurts, but god she's good. She did say I would hurt for a couple of days, but I felt it was worth every penny.

Wednesday 26th February 2014

Today was a good day at work, I felt up, and positive. I was trying to sort stuff out, especially as the surgery was due a CQC visit. I remember thinking how much I love my job, whilst telling Liz what we had done and what needed doing.

Arrived home and found I had missed a call on my phone. It was City Hospital to say they had a slot tomorrow for the operation, as one lady was too poorly to operate. Did I want to go ahead?!I rang poor Simon; it's his birthday tomorrow, but he wants me to go ahead, just to get it done sooner. We may even be able to go to Somerset.

The only problem was mum. I hadn't even mentioned that I need an operation, or even that I had a problem at all. Simon and I arranged to go after work. It took us all our time to get into their house because they had gone for a lie down. Simon ribbed them, as they looked like they'd been having a bit of nooky - haha!

At first mum was a bit annoyed that she didn't know I'd even had a problem. She was a bit upset but in the end seemed okay. We tried to laugh it off and make light of it. We then went home to tell Lou and Jon. I think everyone is happier as they are dealing with it all sooner. Now, off to have a shower with my antiseptic scrub.

And so when I need them
They are either dead or hiding away
No one is now coming out to play
Strength is just another weakness of human resolve
Age takes courage, its waters to dissolve

The battering of a human spirit set adrift
When we cling to a life
When your own imagination of love is that true girl, your
wife

I always knew that somewhere deep and lonely inside
I would have to face my inherited failures, with nowhere to
hide
If Sherifoot Lane was our Jerusalem
Then god has set out to hang each and every one of us
The dark satanic mills that accompanied our wedding vows
Now forge an unknown sadness
For the casual observer to browse

The green and pleasant land that we cherish in our hands
Could it turn to autumn colours
Become lost, dry and empty, as fragile as priestly words and
wedding bands
This is written at a beginning not knowing an end
I still have a life, my love, my children to defend

Thursday 27th February 2014

Simon's Birthday, and what a present! We arrived really early with only one or two others waiting. I don't feel too bad sat in initial waiting area with Simon, but then shortly afterwards they called me down. I said a teary goodbye to

Simon, then set off after a nurse down a corridor into the unknown.

The staff were all brilliant, I was told where to take my clothes off, and given a place to sit. I watched the other patients file in one by one as the consultants and registrars and people came to see each of us and introduce themselves. It was such an assortment of people, one lady was having her nipple tattooed on, another young girl was back for a second time (I'm not sure what for) and one black lady arrived late and just kept texting – she didn't seem in any hurry to do anything she was supposed to.

I felt okay, really. Mr Bolega came down to see me and said they would be starting at 9.00am, around 40 minutes away. Hey Ho here we go.

The nurse came and bagged and labelled my clothes, then walked me through to the theatres where a very nice young man asked me to pop on to a trolley. He was lovely, as was the anaesthetist. I jokingly said 'you will look after me' and he said he'd give me a bit more first to make sure I was definitely under. He was so jolly and reassuring.

Cancer the unknown dancing necromancer
Watcher of the dying
Cannula pain in lonely hospital bed
Family failing, torn and waiting
Fears that love however strong
Will sometimes never break the chain
This moving train of death in locomotion

I remember opening my eyes and groaning in pain and someone saying sorry, and probably giving me a shot of morphine. They then wheeled me to a ward of four and all I can remember was feeling in pain higher up in my tummy. I thought it should be lower. My throat was so dry and lots of Nurses were around checking my pulse etc. I just wanted to drink some water as this was the only thing that would take away my dry throat. The Nurses were efficient and kept checking my catheter and pulse and everything. Then the registrar and a junior nurse came to see me to explain how op had gone. Although I knew they had made a larger incision, I didn't expect for one minute what the Registrar was about to tell me.

Apparently the cancer had spread further than expected, and there were cancer cells like grains of sand covering the Omentum. Because I now need a bigger op, which no-one was prepared for, they had decided to stitch me up, put me on a course of chemotherapy, and then re-operate when tumour or cancer had been shrunk.

They delivered this news to me whilst I was on my own and no-one, not even the nurse who was with her, held my hands. And then they couldn't find any tissues. After they left me with curtains closed, I just cried. They said Simon couldn't come any earlier so I then had to wait around for three hours for him to arrive.

Bless him, he'd had a pint in the Old Windmill over the road and bounced in thinking that all was well. All I could say to him was that it hadn't gone to plan and it was worse than we had first thought. Shortly afterwards the Registrar reappeared to explain everything to Simon.

I remember saying to him that a little light had gone out at the end of my tunnel - all of my dreams and plans for our future together had just been wiped out.

We decided to come clean with the kids and mum.

Simon told the kids, and then went to tell Mum and Norman. The next day he bought Lou and Jon to see me and meet with Mr Bolega to talk everything over. They were brave, but so sad.

We received our morsel of misery today
As I watched a part of my children die, fade away
In a cold hospital side room they crushed our little world
Such innocent tears for the one that gave them life
It wounds my soul, do they also deserve this grief
The final cut from a religious belief

God's laughter at their slaughter
Mock a woman, more loving than you the saviour that we
knelt too
A lady that will burden herself with her children's pain
To see those tears die and smiles reign

To those who at present can sleep
Watch your back, watch the dreams you think you can keep
I watched mine dissolve in a single word
Our fall from Avalon is almost complete

When this is done for my sake
Take me and my children, from this computed world
And press ALT DELETE

Later that day Simon bought Mum and Norman to see me, Mum was so brave but so upset, as was Norman. How can this shit happen to such lovely people who never did anyone any harm? Mum prays night and day. Is this fair to her?!

When they left I felt totally exhausted and told Simon to not come back that evening, and that I'd see him on Saturday to collect me and take me home. Bad decision. I wish I had pushed to leave sooner as that evening I was moved to a main ward, and with my catheter removed I spent all night backwards and forwards to the toilet.

The nurses were so brusque when I asked for some pain killers in the middle of the night whilst visiting the loo. One said abruptly to go back to my bed and that she would bring them down. Every time I tried to get out it was painful, I struggled to even sit up and get off the bed. I can't tell you how upset and alone you feel in a ward full of people in the middle of the night. I couldn't wait for morning to come and for Simon to collect me.

Just before visiting time, I was waiting for the doctor to discharge me, write me a sick note then get some drugs from the pharmacy. Tracey, the senior ward nurse came, and was really good, she said the fact that no Macmillan Nurse had been to talk to me was "shit", in a big way.

An Oncology Nurse has since told me that someone should have come to talk to me. Thank goodness Simon and Jon arrived; you have never seen anyone leave a ward quicker. I didn't wait to say goodbye to anyone, all of the nurses bar one had disappeared anyway. I just walked right out.

The funniest thing was a porter with a wheelchair offered to give me a lift, as he could see me struggling. He told us that the main corridor was ¾ of a mile long - bloody nurses should have organised this for me in my opinion.

Arrived home to Louise and hundreds of flowers which she had organised with Simon, poor thing had even run out of vases to put them all in. So glad to be home! I decided to ask

Mum and Norman round who were dying to see me. We had a lovely time, with all of us laughing and chatting as Simon opened his pressies. I feel guilty that I didn't get him a main present, but things rather over took me.

When Mum and Norman left, the children got ready to go out as it was a big night out for them. Simon and I had a quiet night in on the settee, holding hands and chatting. I love him so much.

I can see my heart shatter
I see fragments of it stick to memories of her life
I cling to her essence like a sunset
Willing it not to set
Never to forget her life, our lives
She is my light my complete long shadow

Sunday 2nd March 2014
Rubbish day. I couldn't settle to anything, not even a film. Glad to go to bed.

Friday 7th March 2014
Simon took the day off work, but the kids went in. We had asked Sue and the others round for about 4pm and Sue arrived early armed with homemade pie, roasties, veg and bits to snack on while everyone had a drink. She had got up early to organise it all, Tina bought dips and Denise had bought doughnuts. I can't believe how kind everyone is being. Nigel and Paul took Simon to the pub after they had

eaten some of Sue's sandwiches and sausage plait, while Sue, Tina, Den and I stayed at home to chat.

They were all amazing, Tina was brilliant telling me how her chemo had gone and how once they had cut it out, it was gone. She said chemo was like magic.

Debbie came a bit later in her usual bright and cheery manner, the boys came back and we all had a lovely time. After a while I did get tired so with numerous hugs and kisses and positive comments everyone went off to Sue's where they stayed until pretty late. Apparently Tina, who hates driving and only does left hand turns, drove to Sue's like a maniac shouting at all the young lads on the way in her little convertible Peugeot. Wish I had been with them.

Saturday 8th March 2014
Mum and Norman came early - we chatted lots, It is so easy being with Simon; he is such a positive soul. I think he must have borrowed my Pollyanna hat (note to self it's only on loan and I want it back soon).
Mum was amazing too, telling me to think positive, make the most of everything and how she would be there for us.

After a little while we packed them off and as the kids were still in bed recovering, we decided to drive over to Wolsey Bridge. I am sure they have moved it since we last went, it's bloody miles away! Then we went to the garden centre, but everything was so expensive and I needed the loo as I had tummy pain. Afterwards we walked over the road to an antique place, but I had really bad tummy ache – I think it's probably wind following the op, but it bloody hurts.

Decided to go to the pub where we had been before with the children and I felt better sitting down, with time to contemplate. There was an old chap to the side of us sitting on his own, and I remarked to Simon how that would be him one day. There was also a table of four people in front of us, aged between seventy and eighty. I'd say they were having a lovely time, but I did wonder if I ever really wanted to get old anyway! We left after one drink, Simon would have bought me lunch but I was uncomfortable so we headed home. A bit of a wasted trip really, but never mind.

Simon made lunch and then after resting I decided to sit outside in the sun with Lou. I wrapped myself in a blanket and we had a lovely girlie chat in the sunshine - she is my beautiful sunshine girl.

Went up for a sleep around five-ish, Matt and Ang popped round and they only stayed a short while. Simon was so knackered, that when I woke up he said could he ask Jenny and Bill to come earlier. He looked terrible, really tired and at the end of his tether, the poor thing.

Jenny and Bill arrived around 6.30 to 7.00, as usual I chatted to Jenny who, although brilliant whilst chatting to me about what to expect, got a bit drunk. I love her - she just doesn't come up for air! Simon talked to Bill in the kitchen. I love them both to bits, they are so full on.

That night we had pie, broccoli spears and M&S rosti, compliments of Sue, what a treat.
I sat down in lounge with Lou and Simon to eat it, and this was the best part of the day. It was peace and quiet, and utter bliss.

Sunday 9th March 2014

Had a brilliant nights' sleep, woke feeling in a totally different mood, feeling very up and ready to face the day. Lou drove us to the Fort where she collected new shoes, and then I went to M&S for some stylish comfy trousers. Lou also sorted a new TV which we ordered later that evening.

Then we went to the park, to Wyndley Gate, for a picnic with crisps. The world and his wife were there as it was such a lovely sunny day. Then I went home to rest as Lou and Simon prepared dinner. Simon made an amazing Sunday roast, it was like he was being the Mother hen and taking care of his little chicks.

Monday 10th March 2014

Woke up feeling bright, disinfected the kitchen, put a wash on and generally pottered about, then got ready and Norman drove me and Mum to Debbie's, where she had prepared lunch for us all. Had a super time, even Norman was on his best behaviour. Debbie was lovely to us all, Mum felt she was a genuine person and so kind. I hope Deb adopts them as grandparents.

When we got back Mum and Norman left to allow me to rest and have a sleep, but then the door went and it was Jono's mum. I let her in, she had bought me a card and chocolates, and had obviously cottoned on from Jono that something was wrong, and as she had to rush off for her birthday meal, the hall was where we stood as I filled her in on what was going on. I'm sad I missed hers and Jono's party, as I'm sure we would have enjoyed it - I'm never usually one to miss a shindig! Simon went to see Camel and I think he had a great night. I'm glad he went because he needs to be distracted.

I HAVE MESSED UP MY DIARY, DAYS ALL COCKED UP - BUGGER!

Monday 3rd March 2014
Jon drove me to the Mitchell Centre after a lengthy morning getting ready and he drove at around 28 miles per hour, regardless of who was behind him. I think he thought he was driving Miss Daisy! We ordered cake to share and two coffees, but I had to get Jon to carry the tray over. By the time I sat down I felt tired and vulnerable. Should I have done so much so soon after surgery? What if I had collapsed whilst with Jon? Anyway, none of that happened. We just sat briefly in the café garden while Jon had a fag. I felt quite weepy and remarked on the lovely countryside, and how I wouldn't ride a horse again. Jon retorted with, 'well you weren't exactly riding before!' He looks at life so differently. It's refreshing really, how he thinks about the unfairness of a 12 year old girl also getting cancer. I love his thinking. Not sure where he gets it from.

Tuesday 4th & Wednesday 5th March 2014
Mum and Norman came round, God, I cannot believe how strong she is being, it's almost like it's not even the same Mum. It must be the Prozac.

On Wednesday I felt a bit brighter, Mum still strong, I think Norman is helping her. I'm thinking of seeing some friends on Friday maybe.

Thursday 6th March 2014

The worse day so far!!! I cried nearly all day. I didn't sleep well and was awake from around three or four with tummy pain. Had an appointment with Mr Bolega and Dr Anwar this afternoon, although it seemed like a bit of a waste of time with Bolega as my histology results weren't through. Vanessa, the Macmillan nurse, rang for them. The doctor just wanted to see how I was post op. Vanessa said afterwards that she was quite worried about me and had rung Dr Rees at Hawthorns Surgery.

I saw Dr Anwar after Mr Bolega, who is a great down to earth guy. He explained about the chemo, three sessions (to be confirmed), followed by an op to cut it all out, which is what Bolega had told him. Chemo would hopefully shrink the tumour to help make the operation more successful.

I pushed to know the staging of the cancer, but wish I hadn't bothered. Stage 4, grade 3. SHIT, SHIT, SHIT. Can this get any worse?

I asked Dr Anwar about the ablation that I had done 8 years ago, and if it could have masked any earlier symptoms, which would have warned me sooner of a problem. I will regret that ablation until the day I die. I feel it has unnecessarily shortened my life by around 30 to 40 years.

I will pursue this, not for any financial gain or to sue anyone, but to research how many more women could be at risk following this procedure. I need to find out whom to talk to about this. I might speak to Professor Kate Thomas at Leyhill.

Tuesday 11th March 2014

Jon drove me to the Fort and I bought a new Samsung phone, which took an age but I'm really pleased with it. I also bought mascara from Boots, although I was a bit undecided as to whether to bother as they may all fall out in a week haha! Then I went to H&M with Jon and managed to find me a stool to rest on whilst he tried on an amazing navy jacket. Even he said how fit he looked in it, but I couldn't persuade him to buy it though, even when I offered to pay half. He said he might buy it after pay day, but for now he got a cardi and a couple of long sleeved tops for a weekend in Leeds.

Wednesday 12th March 2014

Today I injected myself for the first time and it went okay. I had an appointment at Good Hope with a nurse called Julie for a pre-chemo assessment, she talked me through what to expect and how I would feel, then I had a blood test and she even pushed me to book a wig fitting! She showed us where I would go for the chemo, it was all a bit daunting but everyone is so lovely.

Thursday 13th March 2014

Mum came early as the nurses were coming to take my stitches out. I had hoped that my nurse from the previous day would come back, but no such luck. Instead I got a nurse who I had not seen before and she had no idea she was removing stitches, not a clue. Mum held my hand tightly while she tugged on the first one and said it was well stuck, then she managed to yank out the next two, but quickly gave up and said they weren't ready and needed another five days. She said she would get someone to look at them on Monday and that they were coming apart and needed longer. I suggested calling the Doctor for a second opinion which she thought was a good idea as I was going away the next day. I was pretty pissed off when she left. I just wanted them OUT. I decided to call the Macmillan Nurses, and they bleeped a wonderful lady from Heartlands called Julie Smith. She said she would be at Good Hope Hospital in the afternoon and to come over at about two.

After much deliberation Mum said she wanted to come with me, so we ate the lovely M&S lunches she had bought and set off on a fun filled trip to the hospital with Norman driving. God forbid. Julie, Vanessa and an oncology nurse from City were there. They were all totally amazing. Julie said the stitches were more than ready to come out, and that maybe the other nurse was not confident with the technique (fucking useless more like). Whilst the oncology nurse started to remove the clips - which she did so easily - the other two nurses talked to my Mum and made her a cup of tea. It was so good to see how it helped mum, she had a little cry but I think she was so glad she had come with me. Simon came to collect us and dropped Mum off at home. I had a bit of a rest then prepared a bit of packing with Simon for Somerset. Excited!

The world and its tides, its currents
Are not for us to understand.
We pull up our trousers, and straighten our ties
We walk out of wooden doors, with wooden souls
To face another day
Hoping that the ache, the emptiness,
Will dissolve, will flow effortlessly away
Give us some breathing room, within this monochrome grey.

The sun, it shines, the moon, it cries.
The gap between is life
With failings and indiscretions, of guilty drunken times
That are remembered in futile, infantile rhymes
While you lie in your bed rebuilding your mind
Those discarded memories, those convenient truths
Leave you searching, scared of the litter you may find.

Unable to reassemble a thought, within your own mind's eye
To reconnect with a life that is letting you die
In careless abandonment for where you will go
But it always knew where I would go
Weak in losing my strength, praying on my feeble mind
Able to pick and fester on what you see ahead
Not what lay behind

I am laid bare
I am laid out without a care
I am laid dead
I am earth, dry earth un-fed
Each day approaching is filled with a silent sadness of dread.

Friday 14th March 2014

I took it slowly in the morning and packed everything but the kitchen sink, needless to say. We picked up a McDonalds before we set off, then I wriggled, writhed and moaned my way down there as I just couldn't get comfortable in the car. We arrived to a lovely reception, it was low key and I wept a little, but not too much.

Mandy took me off for a little chat and sorted rooms. The place was nice but not as clean as usual. It was very cobwebby, a bit cold and lacking, somehow. The bathrooms were nice, but the loo brushes were a bit grimy. Yuk.

I managed a coffee and just about one glass of wine, which lasted all night. I went up to sit in Tina's room while she unpacked and Mandy joined us. Tina, she is a card. She had bought loads of new clothes which she unpacked and repacked, Mandy and I took the mick, we didn't realise how much she hated spiders and although she was boiling hot she wouldn't open the windows. Supper was pasties from Cornwall and chips, not as good as previous times, they just didn't have any flavour, and no gravy, and it was just lots of pastry. Simon was hungry and had heartburn. It was good conversation after dinner. Simon really enjoyed that bit, and then sat down for a short quiz. Everyone was quite tired and sleepy so we turned in early. Also, it was bloody cold. Debbie and I sat under Lou's sleeping bag all night. Will have to sort that out for Saturday.

Saturday 15th March 2015

After a lovely breakfast cooked by the boys, Simon and I set off to Taunton. After seeing the horses and being given a bit of history about the barn from the owner, we did a quick shop at Tesco then had a mooch around the town. What a great place, there's something for everyone. I would like to come back.

Louise had missed her train and had to pay an extra £47, we finally found her at the station by which time Simon was a bit grumpy (probably hungry) and the traffic was awful. Anyway by the time we got back he had settled down and Louise slotted in a treat. The weather was stunning, though cold, and we all sat outside enjoying scones, jam and clotted cream, compliments of Mandy and Mike.

That evening we had a beautiful curry, we all enjoyed ours, some of the girls didn't like the chicken but we all did, it was delicious. Then we settled down to a quiz which Lou, bless her, excelled at. It was lovely that she now fitted in really well. Unfortunately then we put a film on, which I really wanted to see, it was called "The Secret Life of Walter Mitty", but it bought the whole mood down. Deb and Tina went to bed, followed by us. Simon had a bit of a rant in bed as the evening had slowed down a bit; Lou was so worried the others would hear. The bed was so big, and Lou eventually slept with us as she said her blow up bed was going down. Nice cuddles.

Sunday 16th March 2014
I awoke early and Deb came in for a chat, followed by Tina who was hilarious. She remarked on her hair which was all over the shop and how she was really pissed off that the evening sort of ground to a halt last night. She was hysterical. We decided to go to a car boot with some of the others so we had breakfast and set off. The car boot was so much fun, we all bought items for less than £2 to sell on eBay to raise a bit

of money for a charity that Sue and Paul are involved with. What a laugh! We were all so competitive, I bought two plates with Fergie and Andrew on and a Thomas the Tank toy (Caroline). Lou bought a Wedgewood plate, which she decided to keep, and Simon got a small book on the Brighton Pavilion. Sue listed them all on eBay; it was all so much fun.

Sunday dinner was all going wrong, and Simon was contemplating the long drive home, so we made our farewells and left around tea time. It was a horrendous journey home, the sat-nav had somehow reverted to avoid motorways and it took us about four hours to get back. Ugh! We stopped in the Park Hotel for a carvery, which was expensive and shit, but it filled a gap. I couldn't wait to get home and into bed.

Monday 17th March 2014
A pleasant but tiring day. Simon cut lawns, then we went for a drive, rushed back, rested briefly, then back to Hospital for scan. We were knackered before we even started. Simon was so good, he told me when and how much of this vile aniseed drink I was supposed to have as well as water. He was so lovely. The nurse was wonderful, I felt a bit weepy and she talked to me for ages and told Simon he needed to buy me perfume, and at least two bottles. When we left she gave me a big hug.

Tuesday 18th March 2014

A rubbish day. I had windy tummy pains, and the rest. Felt tired, weepy, and just plain crap. Cried to Simon, Mum and Lou.

Wednesday 19th March

1st CHEMO DAY

The nurses were very kind. Simon stayed for a while to settle me in. It was all done by intravenous which was fine, but the cold cap I had to wear to prevent hair loss was awful. She put it on at 8.30am and took it off at 3.30pm, it was sheer hell, so tight and painful around my forehead. I think the nurse thought she would leave it on as long as possible. Helen arrived to keep me company, we had such a great time, bizarrely. Chatting and catching up, she does make me laugh, we unplugged me when I went to the loo, and then plugged me back in. She wrapped me up and made me laugh and if it wasn't for the cold cap I would even go as far to say I enjoyed the day! Result. Left at 4pm when Jon collected me. It felt great getting lots of phone calls and texts.

Thursday 20th March 2014

Today was a good day, I woke on a high and got mum round to cheer her up. Jon took me to Costco and made me laugh, then later on he made me a delicious, tuna, rocket and cucumber sandwich. Yum.

Friday 21st March 2014

I woke early with crampy tummy ache and was feeling weepy. I talked to Lou about wills, beds and hair! We sorted flowers and I went back to bed. I spoke to Vanessa as my tummy was quite uncomfortable. She wasn't too worried and I continued with pain killers.

Saturday 22nd March 2014
Still got tummy pain so sent Simon off to a record fair. After lots of phone calls the Badger Clinic asked me to go down to see them. Brilliant. Dr Mannan saw me, I think he used to see Mum and Norman at the Jockey Road Surgery. He covered everything, and was concerned I could have something going on as my blood pressure was low. City Hospital asked me to go to A&E.
I rang Simon who was on his way home, and so we both set off for City, then I was finally admitted around 6pm. The nurses were all good and the registrar covered everything, then spoke to a consultant Miss Sundar who prescribed tablets for cramping. I felt safe, the morphine and tablets eased pain. I slept okay, feeling safe.

Sunday 23rd March 2014
I woke early, starving, so I ate cake from previous day then waited for breakfast. I texted everyone as I was feeling great, the pain was sorted and I wanted to go home. Breakfast of weetabix and toast, then a nurse asked me if I could eat a roast beef dinner - I nearly took her arm off!!! Had a chat with Miss Sundar who said I had got a fight on my hands. She was interested as figures for this kind of endometrial cancer have risen from 5 to 15%. I told her I would be interested in travelling to take part in medical trials, so she said she would email Mr Bolega and Dr Anwar in regards to

further testing which had been considered. She also wrote down some info for me to peruse with the consultant. Lou and Simon collected me, had a nice dinner and rested, but then I fell asleep on settee and woke up late feeling really awful.

Monday, Tuesday &Wednesday 24th to 26th March 2014.
Oh my God! Woke up feeling horrendous, there was pain everywhere like a virus, but more painful. Feeling tired and low. I cannot explain how horrible I feel. It's like being run over by a steam roller.

A slow, slow recovery by Wednesday. Simon took me in the car to the Tame Otter pub; we walked up a muddy path by the side of the canal, then popped in the pub and sat in a corner. I just keep crying all the time. Feel oh so low.

Thursday 27th March 2014
Pretty good day though still feel weepy, Mum wants me to speak to Vanessa for some moral support, could not get hold of her but promised Mum I would keep trying. Decided to go out with Jon to Currys to buy a new Dyson. We did have a laugh trying out the "actions". We bought Lou an aerial then went to Ikea. I'm so knackered. I thought Jon was going to buy a teddy he liked which was so soft, anyway, we left with nothing and had to run to car as it was pouring with icy cold rain and needless to say I had no coat on. We came home on the M6, and it was Jon's first time on the motorway with the rain pouring down and my little car steaming up inside. This was not one of my better suggestions but Jon held his nerve. I felt I had rather overdone it by the time we got home.

Friday 28th March 2014

I had a great day with friends overall but again, I'm bloody tired. Liz Collins came to see me with a lovely gift of chocolates and an overnight bag for my next hospital visit. We talked about everything that was going on at work. As soon as she came my mood lifted immediately and I had a lovely time (I didn't know she liked me so much). Denise was scheduled to come at 2pm. Again, great conversation but I felt a bit on edge and quite weepy. While Denise was here Vanessa called and was brilliant, she said she could refer me but that there is an eight week wait. She said I could talk to her at any time. Whatever she said seemed to lift me, and I arranged to see her the following Tuesday after the wig lady.

That evening Simon went to the Vesey for Paul's birthday, I wasn't up for it and didn't think it was a good idea mixing in a crowded pub. Debbie offered to stay with me while Simon and Colin went down to have a drink. Think Deb was rather worried about me as I was so weepy on the Wednesday when she popped in. I said to Deb I didn't want to talk about cancer and on the whole we didn't. I enjoyed the evening but was so tired by the time the boys came back, although it was right on cue at around 9.20pm. I'm so glad Simon had been out, and he said how lovely everyone was.

Saturday 29th March 2014

Simon and Jon at work today. I had a lovely day with Lou, she was a delight, we sat in the sun for a bit although it was bloody chilly. She said she would pluck my chin, five days on and they're falling out on their own. Louise did the sweetest thing whilst plucking my hairs; she kissed me, out of the blue. It was such a lovely gesture full of loads of love; it meant the world to me.

Later on we walked into Boldmere to try and sort Nanny's Mother's day pressie. I wanted to get her a pen after all the drama of the Pound Shop pen that Norman had got her! I felt like a pensioner in Boldmere, slow and uncoordinated. But Lou did make me laugh; she suggested I buy a new nail varnish, then said 'what colour goes with cancer?' If you don't like black humour you won't get this, but it did make me laugh.

We plumped for purpley/pink but there was nothing in Boldmere so Simon drove us to Sutton and while he and Lou drove round the block I eventually found a perfect pen from Smart Ideas. It was £15 but she can keep it after I have gone.

Bumped into Christine Dowd who is a lovely, lovely lady. There were lots of hugs and kisses. I felt like a complete fraud off work sick and trotting around Sutton.

Had a relaxing evening in with Simon, he was completely shattered and we couldn't settle on a film or anything to watch. I felt a bit sad that I hadn't been out for around five weeks. Is this my new life, no parties or evenings out to look forward to?

Sunday 30th March 2014, Mother's Day

Amazingly lovely day, sadly Jon had to work but Doreen and Norman came round and we had sparkling wine, roasted veg tarts and nibbles that she had bought, followed by carrot cake and angel cakes, which are Louise's favourite apparently. They didn't stay too long as they thought I was going to rest, but I was all dressed up in one of my new dresses (nicknamed "The Cancer Collection" by Lou) but with nowhere to go. We decided to set off for the Three French Hens so Lou could practice her driving. She drove brilliantly and once we were there we saw the resident, and ugliest, pig with his very lop sided face. We then went into one of the shops and met someone who worked as a YTS on the style department when I was a manager at Beatties department store. God, how good she made me feel. She said I hadn't changed a bit (I'm sure I had) and how she thought I was still as glamorous. She then proceeded to fill us in on who was doing what from the Beatties good old days. Apparently Paul Woodward had been very ill fighting cancer too. In a ridiculous way this almost helped me, like being part of an exclusive club. At least we won't live to be old, grey and doddery, but will be remembered at the age we die – young!

After leaving Simon suggested we take a look at Swinfen Hall, where we got married. Once we were down the drive he offered to take us in for a drink. He didn't have to ask twice, Lou and I were there like a shot. The place hadn't really changed much and Lou remarked how the colour scheme was the same as our house, haha. We had coffee and homemade biscuits and felt very posh just relaxing and people watching.

That evening Simon and Lou started dinner. Unfortunately I had gone right off, needed pain killers and a hot water bottle for my tummy. I ached everywhere again. Lou and Simon were so on form, quipping and cavorting around the kitchen making dinner. They can be such a delight when they are getting on. Lovely Jon finally came home and we had a fab lamb dinner, then settled down to watch "Meet the Millers". It was a brill film which we all enjoyed, except Simon who snored his way through it.

The children bought me a necklace with all three of their birth stones on, so that they could always be close to my heart. The sentiment behind this chokes me every time; I try to tell everyone about it.

We now stand wide awake in front of a former life
We have to bow our heads and stare into its void
Where the sun will now decide if it wants to shine
And warm our weakened souls

Where the wind will, as my Father once said
Only rustle the leaves of merriment
If it can spare the breath
The stars that shone so bright are dimmed
As we track our journeys course

Am I playing at the edges of the illness of my love
Thinking that my kindness will see her through?
As her body struggles I too must suffer,
Make a change from middle aged comfort
To a raw life, its pain, its heat of thought
Its uncontrollable course.

I found someone who recognised the broken child inside the
man
And now I need to be that whole being,
this husband that lay asleep in the world.
When shops close paradise
And the swell of humanity is met
In waiting rooms and bedside chairs.
We realise we have both been thrust from sanctuary
Into the pit of wanton survival
Where before, a belief in our own invincible, impenetrable
life
Has been shattered, and we clutch at the shards of a former
existence.

The flux of our lives strays between
Warm memory and cold infirmary.
An egg has been thrown against a wall of former belief
Tarnished now by all we scrawled, all we wrote upon it,
All that we hold so close so dear
A path now held in a dust bowl of blown former footprints.

I thought that only my true love knew my innocence
But our lives are now shared at the altar of tawdry grief
Pay the redeemer, feed the thief
We will both be touched, almost marked, stained with this
thin vale of death
One step to the real, but always walking in shadow
Of the former glow of a life,
Washed but now lost in the relentless pouring rain.

Monday 31st March 2014

Rang Allison Sweetnam.We had not spoken properly for a long time and she was so very nice and kind. Felt tired all day, Dawn cancelled as her dog was poorly and I put Mum off and just rested all day.

Highlight of the day was a walk in the park with Simon in the early evening; I felt as though I was filling my lungs with oxygen.

Tuesday 1st April 2014

Moved into our house 16 years ago today. I'll never forget the excitement of showing it off to our parents and drinking Cava in the garden on what was a beautiful spring day.

Lisa Spinks came in the morning armed with homemade Victoria Sponge. I wish mine would rise as well as hers. Had a lovely chat with her about old times, as Simon said, it's a funny old world -

he knew her first years ago when they lived in Sherifoot Lane and how odd that we now worked together and were having coffee.

Hospital appointment in the afternoon, felt really good mentally as the sun was shining, and I had my sunglasses on. Jon sorted out a 90's tape for the car which was fun and didn't make me cry.

The wig fitting was a good experience, not depressing at all. A lovely lady helped us choose a shortish choppy wig which we ordered with highlights. Hopefully it will match my own colouring. I'm still not sure I will wear it.

But now, a week on and my hair is starting to fall out massively so I think I might just need it. Saw Vanessa who had all the time in the world for me, Jon thought she was lovely and to be far she jumped through hoops to get me seen by the registrar about the continuing pain in my side. The registrar completely put my mind at rest, said she wasn't concerned at all it was purely post-surgery pain.

After two hours we finally left the hospital and were starving so Jon and I went to the Horse and Jockey for a late lunch. I had a steak, Jon had a burger and we had a good chat, what a lovely day! Sadly, Simon was on a bit of a downer that evening, work bothering him amongst other things, we did manage a walk and I let him rant a bit, he is entitled to his off days and he must be sick of listening to me moaning on.

Wednesday 2nd to Friday 4th April 2014
Lots of lovely friends and good days. Saw Mum and Norman, Kathy and Allison who were both quite emotional. Sue and Dawn who stayed for ages but did make me laugh, met Jenny again at Dubella, think I am going to book a regular table there!

Can't say enough how supportive and generous people have been, still cannot believe how many friends have come to our aid under such shit circumstances.

Saturday 5th April 2014
How funny! Simon and I were heading out for the day. Simon knocks on Lou's door to say goodbye and who should be in Lou's bed but Marc. Simon creased me up, "oh hello" he said, completely not expecting him to be there. Apparently he hadn't got the message about me and was clueless as to

why Louise was blanking him and had flown home early from his ski season with a broken pelvis.

As he said, did Lou really think he would deliberately ignore a text like that, and to be fair I didn't think he was that kind of lad.

Anyway, brill day out with Simon though freezing cold all day, we went to Moseley Hall and had a fantastic guide who was humorous and informative, though he did have hideous long nails. He told us loads of old sayings and their origins, we had tea cakes and coffee in the café where the National Trust ladies were incredibly slow and confused; at least I won't have that problem if I don't live that long, haha!

Saw a peacock who was incredibly tame, then we set off for Moseley for a bite to eat. I had a tasty steak baguette in a lovely bar where a very nice black lady was wearing a wonderful head scarf with an ornate side knot. I didn't think it was appropriate to ask how it was done though. Set off home as I was really tired, think the cold made me feel achy and crap, had some red wine which made me feel even worse. My hair is coming out in ridiculous amounts, not sure whether to brush, comb or cut it, what to do?

Although I'm not too worried about losing my hair, I felt that now it was falling out I am becoming just like everyone else who had cancer and I would eventually just die like everyone else, so I was a bit weepy. Fortunately Simon found a light hearted film called "Sitter" for us to watch and although I felt a bit fluey again I enjoyed the film with him. Anyway, onwards and upwards.

Sunday 6th April 2014

Gosh, where is time going? Had a lovely day with Simon, after preparing dinner and dropping Jon at work, Simon put my pansies in for me then we decided to go for a walk up the canal by the Dog and Doublet pub. It was not great weather but at least it was dry, had a pretty long walk and so windy, we did laugh as thought I'd have no hair by the time we got back. Enjoyed a lovely glass of red wine and although got a bit upset, told Simon what I wanted for my funeral, he suggested it was a humanist funeral with lots of colour (yellow), to celebrate how much I loved life. I felt angry at having to die so young, felt really close to him. I love his company and the fact that he listens to me.

Drove to Shustoke to another lovely pub where a guy who had walked from the other side of Birmingham, bloody miles, offered us his seat. Set off for home where Simon had to finish dinner as the amount of hair I was losing was crazy.

Lou wasn't happy when she got back home and didn't want to talk. I think she's not sure what to do about Marc as he is going back to do another ski season and I suppose she wonders, what is the point? She and Simon went off to bed early. Surprisingly I felt okay so stayed up for a bit 'til Jon came home. Simon then came back down. He gets so annoyed with Lou when all we get is the leftovers from her boozy weekend.

Monday 7th April 2014

Quiet day on my own, Hilary had to cancel as she had a sore throat. Louise Small came in the evening, lovely to see her she is such a breath of fresh air, just like her mum.

Tuesday 8th April 2014

Good job I've got a wig fitting today, virtually all of my hair has come out. I felt weepy nearly all day - I didn't think losing my hair would upset me so much. Went on my own to the Hospital, after looking on the internet where I found a great way to tie my scarf, and then set off. I felt okay but vulnerable and I must have looked okay because a couple of ladies were commenting on my scarf in the waiting room. I think they were positive. Had a little cry with the wig lady but soon recovered and I am really pleased with the wig. I asked her to walk me out to reception as felt silly walking past the ladies who had just seen me sporting a scarf.

Got home just in time to check hair and makeup before Sue and Paul arrived to drive me to the pub. Had a lovely time though my wig kept riding up which was really annoying. Will have to super glue it down maybe. Felt I was a bit quiet but did enjoy it and the girls were lovely as usual but then again I was bit weepy later on.

(Back to Monday 7th April)

Woke up with a mohican hair style (not so cool) and had two big mats of hair which were gross! Had a shower and virtually all of my hair ended up in the shower tray. I had booked a haircut for today but by the time I got out of the shower I asked Jon and we decided to just cut it ourselves.

Looked okay, quite elfish really and felt loads better. No more hairs in my dinner anymore.

Wednesday 9th April 2014

2nd CHEMO DAY

Simon collected me then Mum, think she was a bit apprehensive but she's one strong lady. After they got things underway and I had got mum off the subject of cancer, we had a laugh. The young Nurse thought mum was making notes on the questions she had asked her, but no, mum was filling in the crossword! We did manage to polish off the walnuts and ginger she had bought which were delicious. She made me laugh as she was tucking in; think she was quite disappointed when she had to leave.

Shortly afterwards Kathy arrived, it all became a bit fraught as when they put up my second lot of chemo treatment, and it was scary really; I was talking to Kathy and felt a funny sensation in my throat and chest then suddenly the onset of shooting pains in my lower back which happened really quickly and scarily. It got very bad, three nurses came over and stopped the chemo, and they put fluids back on and rang Dr Anwar. After a while things settled down, then after checking obs and getting the okay from the registrar they restarted the chemo at a slower rate. I did ask Kathy if she was any good at CPR!

Once they had restarted the pain in my back had stopped but it was really uncomfortable and after a bit of tweaking and a heat pad everything was calm, thank goodness.

Finally had a lovely chat with Kathy although as usual we flitted all over the place and it took my mind off everything. We have so much in common,

Vanessa came briefly with some more info, then Simon, Kathy and I left together but not until 6.30pm. I was the last patient to leave.

Got home and felt weary. I had cabin fever so went for a walk around the block with Simon, then we all settled down to watch the film "Liberace". It was a bit weird but okay. Weary now, bed please.

Thursday 10th April 2014
Woke up feeling really good made two ratatouilles, cleaned, put some washing on then got ready for the district nurse, Lorna, to visit. Lovely lady, had a really good chat about her role and what she could do for me. I still keep thinking it feels like palliative or end of life care but hey ho! Simon came home from work and we set off for the hospital to see Mr Bolega. Had really good banter and a laugh with Simon. It was outrageous really, black humour at its best and I don't think Vanessa the Macmillan nurse can quite work us out.

Mr Bolega was lovely as usual and positive. He wants to go ahead with surgery as soon as possible. The plan is third chemo then wait three weeks, then have a CT scan. He will book op then review the scan and if necessary more chemo, he did say that the previous CT scan showed that my chest was clear, he also said I was rare and unique, well, at least my cancer was. He said not to look on the Internet as no statistics would be relevant to me. Left on a high for once.

Went for a walk around the block with Simon which always helps me sleep better. I collected Lou from the train station whilst Simon cut the lawns. Lou was a bit upset as had rung Marc about Saturday and didn't feel the relationship had legs. I think she was annoyed with me, we were at logger heads all evening sadly.

Friday 11th April 2014

Mum came early-ish and loved my wig, sorted out Norman's prescription and set off to Sainsbury's and T.K.maxx. We found four lovely scarves, and had to laugh while trying on a sunhat over my wig. Suddenly there were lots of people all around me and I had to ask mum to remove the hat whilst I held on to my wig, so funny! Had a good lunch with Mum and Norm. I showed her my bare head; she was so brave and said it wasn't too bad at all. I hardly think Norman noticed.

Mum put my wig on top of her own hair; she can be a card at times. I told them how I didn't, sorry, only, wanted to live a good quality of life, (good job I changed that!) and that I don't want to be brain dead, in a wheelchair and doubly incontinent. I spoke candidly about the plans for the funeral, but as ever tinged with humour. They took it all very well, Norman thought I was brave.

In the evening Louise drove us over to Sarah and Richard's for a little drink. It was the first evening out for me since 22nd February. We had a very warm welcome from them both and had a lovely time chatting and catching up on Sarah's party and their trip to Yorkshire. Sarah loved her necklace even though it was weeks late! Great night.

Saturday 12th April 2014

Lazed around pretty much all day, until about 3pm then got ready to pop to Angela and Matt's. We walked there and I felt weary but okay. We didn't stop talking, Matt has put one of Simon's poems to music, and Simon was really pleased. At home later we had a curry and watched a good film.

Sunday 13th April 2014

We decided to buy a tree to fill a gap in the garden that had been there for years, bought a lovely dark green and red Cotoneaster, helped Simon to plant it, and it was a beautiful day, though bloody freezing. Simon worked like a Trojan digging the hole and planting the tree really well to give it a good start, he had also scrubbed the garden swing seat for me for the summer. It was so clean it looked like he had bleached it. We cooked dinner but the evening became a bit disjointed, feel as though we are all avoiding the subject, and all I do when I am with the kids is get upset.

Monday 14th April 2014

Terrible day, cried nearly all day and didn't sleep well as I slept on the settee because Simon was snoring. Nothing or no one would have picked me up.

During the day Simon kept popping in and calling me, in the evening we went for a walk in the park. Again this did pick me up. I must keep going out for these walks as it always lifts my mood.

Booked a break to the Cotswolds and stayed up a bit with Lou, Jon and Simon. It was a better evening and Lou is happier about driving as her lesson went well.

Tuesday 15th to Thursday 17th April 2014

Feel loads better than last chemo and had hardly any painkillers, feel pretty normal. Louise passed her driving test, brilliant, bought her some flowers. So pleased she has passed first time.

Knew she could do it, she had a brill teacher, Mary. Bought her a card and wine, it gives Lou The freedom she needs. That evening Simon bought wine and I put a pizza in, we celebrated Easter with Mum and Norman, think they enjoyed it, we certainly did.

Friday 18th April 2014

Went to Tesco with Simon. Lou came back from a night out and we did the Easter egg hunt. Felt really low whilst getting ready to go to Sue's 50th. Thank goodness for Simon who helped me with my wig and make up and encouraged me to get ready. So glad we went to the party, met up with friends of Sue and Steve's who were at their last barbecue. We had a great time, she was so complimentary telling me how fab I looked, which was amazing seeing as I had earlier nearly melted my wig underneath a patio heater. I felt normal.

Saturday 19th April 2014

Set off for the Cotswolds, it was a beautiful place and hotel with a massive room with a settee and the biggest bed I've ever seen. It was the perfect temperature and clean. Everything we wanted. After a walk around the village we found a sun trap at a pub opposite the hotel, enjoyed a glass of wine whilst crying and talking to Simon. We watched the blackbirds. It was the sort of place you wanted to bottle and freeze in time.

We went back to the hotel for a short rest then got ready in my best dress. I felt great, put my wig on with Simon's help and again he made me feel fab, saying how much he liked the wig. It was amazing food and service, after the meal we found a little spot in a side lounge and played Taboo. The first card I pulled out was wig, so we had a good laugh about that.

Sunday 20th April 2014
Great start to the day, feeling loved and normal. Set off to Hidcote Gardens, it was absolutely freezing and I had to borrow one of Simon's big jumpers. Finished off the day in Bourton on the Water, where the sun finally came out. Then we had another beautiful meal back at the hotel, Simon said I looked like a rock chick in my new top, and he keeps saying how much he loves my hair.

Monday 21st April 2014
Set off to Buscot and had a very long walk along the source of the river Thames and managed to loop back along the road to the car. Set off to a Tithe Barn which dated back to the 13th Century. We sat in the sun for a while, then set off home where Simon cooked a curry and we watched the film "Captain Phillips."

Tuesday 22nd April 2014
Met up with Helen and Kev for a bite to eat at the Jockey, spent a lovely afternoon with them, they are such good company. Watched a strange film in the evening.

Wednesday 23rd to Friday 25th April 2014

Lots of coffees and lunches with friends, all lovely but feel so bored. Need to find a hobby. We spent a lovely evening on Thursday with Mum and Norman for their anniversary. Simon and I had seen Dr Anwar which was all good. The kids drove mum and Norman to the Jockey, all seemed very tense by the time they got to us, goodness knows why! Afterwards they came back to ours and chatted till 10pm, they are good company.

Saturday 26th April 2014

Rested all day, Lou stayed out at Marc's so didn't see her, Jon was around a bit. Off to Tina's tonight, can't wait.

What a lovely evening managed to stay until 1am, felt so normal Colin said I looked fab! And I felt fab. Had a very short dance, nice chilli and super time chatting to Sue, Colin and Paul. It was very relaxing.

Sunday 27th April 2014

Had a lovely lie in, both of us knackered, but got up eventually and went to the park, reasonable walk with the usual hot chocolate stop. An afternoon and evening of films, it was great

Monday 28th April 2014

Woke up feeling really weepy, Hilary collected me and we went to Dubella, had a good time but felt choked and sad all day. Walked in the evening then lay on the settee feeling cold and miserable, told Simon it was best to leave me alone.

you may live longer kneeling in the pews of devotion
But if you glimpse the sun beyond the church wall,
If you look outward from your inherited religion
Look beyond the misers' fire
Warm your hands on your own existence and belief.

Question those old ladies that clutch their Palm Sunday cross
A holy justification for their loss
Hell is visiting us today. It will linger with us tomorrow
Who unlocked the gates and handed us a debt on time to
borrow
It is enjoying and revelling, laughing at our sorrow

When I walk alone my tears mock my footsteps home
To the sanctuary of a now sleeping life
She is my Troy, my strength, my hiding place
She, holding us all within.

A precious other day comes to a close
And I see my world in her eyes
Each drop of her humanity, is a tear within my sight
Although her burden is heavy, she smiles
That spring bouquet, her fragrance of life is my perfume.
So each day we walk, we cling to hope.

Tuesday 29th April 2014

Had a blood test then mum popped to see me, had another good cry. Felt sorry for upsetting them but just couldn't help myself, they did cheer me up though as they were so strong and positive. Angela called to take me for a coffee at the Garden Room, had a good time but felt really tired as it was already 3pm. Ate a delicious Banoffee cake, but afterwards was queasy and achy, left around 5pm and came straight home, had a bath and went to bed. I slept virtually right through, even snored according to Simon. I'm just exhausted.

Wednesday 30th April

Arrived at the hospital only to be told I'd got the wrong date, my fault. Rearranged plans, a lady from St Giles Hospice came at around 11am, she told me everything I was entitled to including a GS1500 form. I couldn't stop crying, this is a form for terminal patients with a life expectancy of six months or less, did some research on the internet and others had said they had lived longer than this, but I can't get my head around the finality of it all. Felt so sad, angry and low. I managed to get around Costco with Mum and Norman. I did tell her that I had a life shortening illness which I do not think she had grasped.

Went to the pub with Simon to drop the bombshell, obviously he was gutted too. Shit night of tears and sadness.

Thursday 1st May 2014
3RD CHEMO DAY
Simon dropped me at the hospital, a lovely young nurse called Becky who had seen me before went to ask about GS1500 form and speak to Vanessa. I felt a bit lifted by what she had found out and she was so kind. Jon came mid-morning and as usual was really good company, doesn't even say anything outstanding but is just so chilled and nice to me. After he had left Vanessa popped to see me and to explain about the GS1500. She said that it was money we are entitled to and that it was automatically filled in for stage four cancer patients and one of her ladies had been renewing it for three years. Wow, so I may get three years.

Kathy arrived around 2pm, as usual great conversation. We do get on so well. Finished at 5pm, Simon collected me and we went for a teary walk, even though news slightly better every step makes me realise how real and crap all this is. Got home and was completely shattered. Jon made me a jacket potato then I went to bed.

Friday 2nd May 2014
Cancelled nails and a visit from Lisa as I was just too tired, lay in bed and I quite enjoyed the rest, but knew I needed to get up. Finally had a bath put nice clothes on and lots of make-up and set off for not sure where really. Asda, St Giles, Ley Hill Surgery? Decided to head to St Giles, needless to say I got lost but finally arrived. It was a beautiful day and glorious setting. Walked in and waited at reception, I immediately filled up and my voice went really hoarse, they were obviously used to this, a lovely lady took me off to a quiet seating area made me coffee and talked to me. She

asked if I wanted to talk to a counsellor, I said yes and so this counsellor took me to a comfy room with soft music. She had one of those soft dreamy kind of voices. They just seem to know exactly what to say.

I was told about all the activities available, and they booked me in to see another counsellor next week, followed by a complimentary massage the following week. A number of the activities appealed to me and I'm so pleased I went. I feel this is a turning point and a new focus, an alternative from numerous cups of coffee and lunches.

When I left I went to shake her hand and she hugged me. She was so lovely, as was the lady on reception. Afterwards I felt really good so went to Simon's office where I had wine and a great chat with them all. I felt really good and so much better than earlier.

Saturday 3rd May 2014

Kids all had their own plans so Simon and I set off for Shackerstone, one of my favourite Leicestershire villages. It was a beautiful sunny day and our usual banter prevailed. We must have been about the only visitors to the village as it was deserted, which suited us just fine. We managed a little round trip of the lanes and canal, and then set off for a look around Market Bosworth which was bustling. We bought ourselves a little picnic reminiscent of those we had in Corfu: cherry tomatoes, fresh bread, avocado, dolcelatte, I think, and salami.

We then found a very upmarket pub/restaurant where we sat outside in the sun for a drink. Earlier, when we arrived to get this drink, there was a group of young attractive blonde women sat outside drinking Prosecco. Simon must have sensed how self-conscious I felt because as we walked past he put his big strong arm around me and pulled me towards him and kissed my head, wig and all. Later as we sat outside an older couple with their son and girlfriend were spouting on about what they had done with their finances for the future, and what a big "I Am" the old guy was. What a pain.

After that we set off to find a picnic spot, which we found just over a bridge on a bend. We parked the car, took our trusty green picnic chairs and sat in the full sun by the side of the canal. There was not a soul about. We ate our lunch, two little souls as one in perfect happiness and harmony. Why does this cruel world have to take that away?

I live with the only constant in my life, my bed
Apart from these words that swarm inside my head
This constant that is my rainbow,
I would freely cast the coins that people search for
In to the pools of lost fortune
For her body to hold within an ever turning hour glass.

Her sleepy face at peace as we lay on a Sunday morn
Remembering those lost lives
The mourning of what has made us real
If I am alone, if you fly home
I hope the salt will blind my empty tear stained eyes
A darkness fills my memory, your hair, your face, your
beauty.

Picture a country path
Bleak desolate trees, reach from the hedgerow
Dark talons against the sky
I will walk that path, memories in hand
A glow captured within my heart
I knew our love. I knew that the end had a start.

I will close the door on breathing love, remember safe
suffocation
Untarnished, pull at the anchor set sail on lonely seas
Turbulent, on the waves of those never to be recaptured days
Shroud me in remembrance skies
For if you have burnt your soul to another love
Life is nothing, life is fragile.
Set free the white flying dove.

Sunday 4th May 2014

I woke feeling okay, if not a little tired. Lou had mentioned going into town to try to find a new dress for this evening. I needed something to wear too so Simon agreed to drive us in quite close, and park the car and then we'd have a brief look around. Lou was worried about leaving me but although I felt a bit wobbly, I said I would be fine. After walking into the first shop I bought a lovely stripy dress then went straight into Next and bought some loose trendy trousers. I couldn't find a top but met up with Simon in Café Rouge and people watched while Lou struggled to find an outfit.

People watching can be strangely therapeutic, watching all shapes and sizes pass by, makes you wonder how many of them have a hidden cancer, yet undetected bursting into life, ready to bite them on the bum in weeks or months!

Arrived home weary but pleased to greet James and Chris who wanted to pop in and see us. We had an excellent time, but not sure if it was such a great idea - it felt as though it was hammering home my inevitable outcome as Irene, Chris's wife, had stage four ovarian cancer. It was all too close for comfort.

Monday 5th May 2014

Got up and did angry cleaning. I felt irritable and annoyed as the house felt like a tip. Poor Simon, if only he is to clean it, he will still disappear under piles of washing, dirty mugs and vacuuming.

When we had finished I felt strangely better, still annoyed with the kids who seem oblivious to keeping the house tidy.

Rang mum and Norman and arranged to go for a walk in Shenstone, and then pop to see Louise and Hayden. It was like taking two excited little children out, they loved the walk. I hope they will do it again on their own.

A pub stop with them is never very successful. Mum didn't know what to order, thinks everyone is toffee nosed and never really enjoys the whole relaxing with a drink experience, especially seeing as it was pretty cold and windy. Anyway, got back to the car and set off for Lou and Hayden's who made us very welcome. My problem is always making sure mum enjoys herself, which she never will. Sadly she lacks confidence and the art of conversation in company, and now with her hearing going I spent more time relaying conversation between mum and auntie Mel than actually relaxing myself, a problem I have had since my dad died I suppose.

Finished the afternoon at home with them, having a drink and a chat. When they had gone I settled down for a quiet evening in, with Lamb Kleftico and a poor quality film.

Tuesday 6th May 2014
Woke feeling awful, flu like symptoms again. Aching from head to toe and terribly weepy. Stayed in bed all day until my scan in the afternoon, as I felt so poorly. Simon rang to see if they'd see me sooner, which they did. Struggled my way through that nasty aniseed drink again which was a real struggle. Simon kept rubbing my back to make me feel better and a nurse took me through for the needle in the arm. She was completely wrong for the job, hair and nail extensions full blue eye make-up - how on earth was she going to get a

needle in me with those long talons? Sure enough, although needle went in okay she couldn't get the fluid through. A colleague then tried and said she would do the other arm. In the meantime whilst she had left me I started being sick and managed to bring up most of the fluid I had drunk.

After a short rest they took me through to scan me, but they were still not happy with the vein they had chosen. So after trying several sites on my arms whilst I lay on the scanner, they called in what I assume was a more senior registrar or radiographer, and while two nurses comforted me and one said how young I looked for my age, the senior Doctor found a vein higher up my arm. They were all very lovely but I was so scared and sad I could hardly stop shaking. Just wanted Simon to take me home. When the scan was finally over, we went home, me to bed and Simon to another lonely night on his own in the lounge.

Wednesday 7th May 2014
Woke still feeling achy and crap, not so upset but feeling really poorly. I cancelled my appointment at cancer support and stayed in bed all day.

Thursday 8th may 2014
Still don't feel great, Mum and Norman came round in the morning and were quite cheery, although I felt really zonked out. The chemo had really knocked me about this time. Set off for the hospital with Simon, we half joked that it was the bad news clinic as it was so quiet. Sure enough it was the bad news clinic; Mr Bolega says that the cancer hasn't shrunk at all following the chemo. In fact it has grown a bit further into

the diaphragm and the spleen. Therefore he isn't going to operate. Quite frankly both of us are devastated. We were both convinced that he would operate at some point. Why had my magic juice not worked like everyone else's?

Simon and I have gone into free fall, this is just like a really bad dream that we will finally awake from and they will say it was all just a nightmare. So hard to take it in, how can I have been so well and now knocking at deaths door?

We were going to try to hold off telling Lou as she was having a really difficult week at work, but the first thing she said when she came in was "has it worked?". We couldn't lie to such a direct question. Poor thing was devastated when we said no. I don't think she knew what to do with herself. Where do you find comfort when there is no comfort anywhere to solve the pain?

Jonathan bounced home and we told him, he cried so much to me and then later with Simon and I on our bed. What is so devastating is that Lou and Jon both said they thought I'd be alright, in our twinkly little special world, where everything has a solution and Mummy and Daddy make everything right. They thought that in the end I would be okay and it would all go back to normal again. Sadly our magic has slipped and crashed around our feet, leaving two little babes with pains in their hearts so bad that it will never go away.

All the irritation and annoyance over stupid little things, like being tidy and helping around the house are brushed aside and what is left is raw love and emotion in its purest form, like the baby love you have for them and they for you, when they are little. The love of a mother when you breastfeed them for the first time, and they look up in your eyes as their protector and carer examining all the details in your face to identify you and bond with you. There is nothing quite like the love a mother has for her children that she has borne from her body.

Now these little children are being sent into the wilderness to fend for themselves like creatures in the wild. Who would do that, and never see their young again? Well that is what I will be doing in weeks, maybe months but not years, to my little children.

I am and always have been a pillar of dust
Sucked dry by this world, bemoaning my chances, my crust.
But I saw her only once, and knew she was and would be my only love.
Trench coat mystery, as she passed my sight
Haberdashery high points, would no longer see me through
Once she, had danced across my plain my view
I was trapped, taken, sold and branded to her heart,
This heart that would see me to the end.

I am now David set to defeat Goliath
To reach an ultimate consuming love and commitment
I have shot my life's weaknesses between the eyes
Watched them fall, watched them roll away
Watched the chains break, reform in somebody's yesterday.
It has left me naked and self harmed
But she held out her small loving hand
And took me to her backwater heart.

Waters that lie so still so deep and true, so calm within
breathing lives
Oh so lucky me, to visit them, bathe in them
After each morn, each night, each returning working day
Chase my selfish consuming troubles away.

She holds a secret, an unknown spell
Entraps not only me, but captures us all
Her butterfly wing, her fleeting glancing mind
So alive of thought and fervour
Each open flower would long for her visit
To feast upon the nectar of her company.
She, in some strange wonderful way pollinates us all
With her honesty and humble beauty
Each meeting enhanced by her voice, her smile, her sweet
charm.

Friday 9th May 2014

Couldn't decide how to break the news to Mum and Norman,
Simon was going to tell her on the phone, but then we
thought about it, and decided we had better get her round.

In the end I gave an Oscar winning performance, and just
emphasised that they were going to try different treatments,
but not operate. Of course she knew I wasn't telling her
everything. She popped in again before we were due to go to
St Giles Hospice. We told them pretty much everything and
she was so upset. Simon did his best to comfort her but she
was trying so hard not to lose control, I decided it would be a
good idea for them to come with us to see the counsellor at St
Giles with me.

In between all of this Sue Brown was on her way back from the dentist, she said she couldn't keep away and just wanted to see us. Her big warm hug enveloped me and her words lifted us both up. She said at least she could tell Paul we were okay. She just wanted to see us and be with us herself. My description of what she did is crap, but thank you Sue for just bringing a small bit of light into that sad day for us, manky mouth and all from the dentist.

St Giles were lovely, although two of the counsellors were a bit useless they at least got mum to open up a bit. But the gaps whilst they waited for you to talk seemed ridiculously long. I felt better when they took me off for a while so that Mum could talk, and Elly could speak to me on my own. I don't know what she said but at some point that afternoon she made me realise that now I had to put myself, Simon, Lou and Jon first. Mum and Norman had lived a very lovely life together, but now my emphasis was on my little family. I feel I had almost put too much emphasis on my Mum, to the detriment of Simon. It was like a light bulb moment when I realised I needed to be selfish moving forward. I came away from St Giles feeling brighter and more positive in some strange way.

The funniest thing, while we were talking to the two counsellors I could see Simon outside with his headphones in and a book under his arm. He looked as though he was pacing out the acreage of some estate in a ridiculous way. It was like a comedy sketch going on outside the window, while we were trying to have a serious discussion inside. It makes me laugh just to think of it.

Once mum and Norman had left we decided to go to Miller and Carter to use up Simon's voucher from work. How odd was this, to just paper over the cracks and blot out the shit that was about to hit the fan. Although it was my idea, I found it hard to eat and stop my mind wandering off into the land of dark thoughts. The Prosecco helped though!

Saturday 10th May 2014
How strange the mind is, to absorb such awful news, then come to terms with it and yet move forward. Once Jon had gone to work, Lou, Simon and I decided to go to Solihull, more so I think because Louise had said the previous night that we would never go shopping again. Well there was no way I was having that, so there we were in Solihull.

The weather was really good but I think that was because the wind was so strong it was blowing all the rain clouds away. As we walked out of Beatties towards the centre the wind was almost like a hurricane and the three of us nearly wet ourselves as I clung on to my wig, which I had forgotten to tape down in our hurry to leave the house.

How strange that while inside it feels as though your heart is breaking, you can still find humour in such ridiculous things. I hope you can all look back and remember this in years to come, with the same laughter as we all felt that afternoon.

Felt a bit weary while shopping but managed to buy my favourite perfume, bizarrely called "Happy" although after spraying it liberally over myself, I'm not sure if I've gone off it. Went for a bite to eat at Wetherspoons, and while Louise and Simon tucked into their super food salads, I tucked into burger, chips and extra mayonnaise. Well it was too late for me now.

That evening, we were due to go to Debbie and Colin's Eurovision evening for Colin's 60th, and although I had slept, I woke quite late and didn't really feel up to it. Nevertheless, we dutifully got ready and set off armed with Prosecco for courage. Everyone was lovely and chilled when we arrived, no pitying looks just normal welcomes from them all, I was then able to slip on to a settee beside Denise and lose myself in her chatter and the TV programme.

Sue made me laugh when she shouted to Denise to "shut the fuck up" as she was talking non-stop and not paying attention to the programme. Poor Denise, she did seem to shut up for a while then.

When all the songs had been sung the girls came to chat to me, Tina on one side, Sue the other and Liz on the floor. It was like having a big extended family all around to give a supportive hug. The fun all of us had planned will just go ahead without me, and it can only be a good thing for Simon, to have this lovely group of friends who I know will be so supportive in months to come.

Who would have known that they would embrace us so warmly into their group on our first holiday to Anglesey with them? What a laugh they thought we were cavorting on the beach with a kite, whilst at night Simon coughed incessantly with the most irritating tickley cough. I was a right miserable bugger, as I was not getting enough sleep, but they obviously liked us, and loved Simon when he had us all waving loo roll while singing along to Mama Mia on the Saturday night.

Anyway, back to Eurovision Night. After a couple of hours we decided to leave, I was tired and a bit emotional, so we made our excuses. Paul was so lovely to me in the Kitchen offering to help or do anything he could, all we had to do was ask. As everyone came to say goodbye, I just wanted to leave as quickly as possible. It was all so hard to say goodbye, just feels like every time is going to be the last time.

Sunday 11th May 2014

As usual we woke up early and decided to make a list of things we needed to do, even in the face of adversity, we still felt the need to make a list. Decided to go for a walk in the park and then pop to see Angela and Matt who were going away the next day. What a lovely hour or so we spent with them, I completely lost myself in their holiday plans. When we came back I looked through our photos of Rome, but disappointingly none of them could describe how close the Colosseum was to the Forum and everything else that was there.

Monday 12th May 2014

Simon set off to meet Lee and Paul, his bosses, to discuss the plans for the next few months. They said they were thinking of viewing it as paternity leave. I think he really enjoyed seeing everyone at the Walmley Office as well.

The labour of dying
Was met with the keepers of Bedlam and Babel.
To plead for a life, set adrift now unstable,
I set off carrying my grief so bright upon my smart cuffed
sleeve,
My heart set to wage freedom against the balance of profit
and loss.
Their loss.
They hold the hammer, they forge the nails.
They could turn the rack to stretch our lives
But when the keeper of the key
Shook me by the hand in mutual respect, to reconcile the
hurt, the imminent loss,
My heart was stabbed with guilt
And my mind was washed with hope
For I said we were all done for within this company,
We minions, we faceless, you and me.
Remember the cut, the ones they set aside?
It was said to those remaining, someone would remember
where we stood
On the turning of the tide.

So we laboured forth, we believed in human resolve.
We possibly believed in love and kinship,
A friendship forged within the working maze
Those corridors to run, happiness in a day's work done.

But avarice can take and strike any man
Even the most curious and truthful hearts
Can without knowing be absorbed. Let each day distort their
view
Become judge and jury in a profit led court
Until lost in the single language of Babel

Mad and self believing, as those lonely souls in Bedlams
stable.

But I believe what passed in that handshake
Between the cornered poacher and the keeper
Sparked a sense of humanity in each.
The poacher knew the game was run
The keeper saw himself, if facing the dark barrel of a gun
A split seconds freedom from all that ties us down
From our Bedlam and our Babel
Understanding realised, and madness put aside
Thank you.

While Simon was out Mum and Norman popped in and once
again they seem to have pulled themselves together and are
looking at the positives with us.

That afternoon Louise left work early and Viv Forester from
St Giles came out to see us. Although a lovely lady, I didn't
feel the same warmth from her that I felt from "Bin", but by
the end of the afternoon I had warmed to her, and she did
make me feel a bit happier when she said one out of three
patients don't get any pain, and that I will just start to slow
down. Lou and Simon felt she was really helpful.

Tuesday 13th May 2014
Had arranged to meet Marie and Lisa from work at the
Speckled Hen and although I had considered cancelling after
the last lot of bad news, I decided as I was still alive and

wasn't entertaining dying very soon, that I would go anyway. I'm so pleased I did. Julia picked me up and arrived around 1.30pm. Amanda and Jill were there to meet me and slowly a few others arrived - Dawn, Lee (Lisa), Anne, Lisa and Marie.

We ordered cake and drinks and I held court; no tears were shed and I felt strong and wanted to tell the girls not to ignore any symptoms they may ever have, however insignificant. We chatted easily for a couple of hours and afterwards Julia said we should pop in to see if anyone was in at the admin office at the surgery. Only Debbie, Amy and Lynda were in, but they were really pleased to see me. Poor Lynda was finishing that day for another knee op, and we joked that I could move into her office to do some work, and she would make sure no boxes were hanging around (in joke).

Julia then said we should go to the surgery next door, but through the back entrance, so hopefully I wouldn't catch anything. In there I saw Pauline and Gillian who filled up a bit, Liz, Wendy and then Marie and Anita. Two nurses from upstairs came down too. They all said I looked amazing, and I felt it too.

On the way home in the car Dawn text me too apologise profusely for her previous text. When I looked at my phone she had apparently text Neil, her husband, to say I only have six months to live, but had sent it to me instead! She must have been mortified. Told her not to worry and that she was only repeating what I had told her (according to the DS1500 form). I then wiped the message and I didn't mention it to Julia, poor Dawn.

Julia kindly dropped me home and had left a lovely gift of lavender spray and temple salve for me. Julia is a lovely, lovely lady. That evening Simon and I went for a walk in the park. I went to bed exhausted.

Wednesday 14th May 2014
Simon is now officially off on long term leave with me, whether he will ever go back remains to be seen but he will never be the valuer at Walmley office again. Although I always talked to Simon about dropping Saturdays or working part-time, he used to say it would never happen. How wrong he was! Yet again I am right. See, told you I'd sort it for you!

So on that Wednesday morning we set off on our early fast forward retirement plan. We bought a juicer, Jon had gone on about how we should all eat like bunnies, and not buy into the whole Tesco shopping and chemo as cancer treatment thing, that it was all a conspiracy theory. Coincidentally I had rung my hairdresser to ask advice about my straggly hair, although she advised me not to have a haircut. She told me that her and her sister had taken their mother, who had cancer, out to Mexico to follow a strict diet to help control her illness. She reckoned it had prolonged her life by twelve months, and if I wanted any help or advice just to contact her.

Maybe fate had made me ring her that morning but somehow it felt right, so there we were in John Lewis spending £144 on a juicer, the Sage one she had recommended. Then we set off to two farm shops in Tamworth for fruit and veg. Unfortunately we live in a country that imports such a lot of our produce, and we still ended up buying Spanish tomatoes and a number of other imported fruits and veg. Nevertheless we were trying our best!

After a chance stop to see some Piggies who were careering around the fields near Hopwas, we also stopped at another farm shop for a coffee then had fun with Simon in the garden centre choosing a rose bush for Mum's birthday. Some of the names were ridiculous; Sexy Rexy and Seductive Lady for example. Then we went home to make juice.

That afternoon Helen came and we spent a couple of hours in the garden in the sun, chatting and laughing. It was a lovely afternoon. Helen encouraged me to continue with my journal, including all the funny little anecdotes, so that they could be read in the future. I did tell her it would never make the best seller list as it is very droll and boring! English never was my forte.

So we have our retirement on speed,
A retirement so fast, not captured within the shutter's eye,
Too fast for thought, but long enough to absorb the anguish.
Each pulse, each twinge within her body
Each passing day, the beginning of the fading away.

Each smile is tinged, stained with the knowledge of parting.
The unstoppable inevitable loss.
Our children
The new found alchemist and the eternal tearful optimist
They are the bonnet, windscreen casualties here
As their bodies role within the detached air of an abnormal
life.

Their tears spit and spatter their anger
Against the shattered glass of yesterday.
The tarmac may break their fall, but they are buried through
the black.
A grief so dark, for a Mother's touch, tears and smile
Will they dare, with broken hearts, look back?

I will carry their strain, pack it safely with my own,
I may be consistently boring, but Lord I was built for pain.
So bring on your so called 'release',
Bring on your silent kingdom, your never understood peace,
Bring on my hives, bring on hell on earth, we shall endure.
For humanity and its love
Is stronger than any religion, and its promise
A hollow belief now sits aside our growing grief.

The mobile family photo holds no negative,
How apt is that?
No alternate view, no yesterdays today
No dark image, just life held within the click, that technology
trick.
What you see in a moment of light
Four smiles, four hearts, four pasts.
Three futures. Now unknown, and unclear.

Thursday 15th May 2014
Had my nails done very early and collected the car from
servicing. It was Mum's birthday so we said we would meet
her after seeing Dr Anwar about the way forward. Waited
one and a half hours before we were seen. Mr Bolega popped

his head out to mention something about a medical trial and then when we finally went in to the appointment, we felt slightly more optimistic than we had since the appointment with Mr Bolega the previous week.

Dr Anwar's language to us was far more positive; he explained about the trial and also about hormone therapy. I asked him what, god forbid, he would do if it was a member of his family and he said he would go for the medical trial. Simon still wanted to narrow down how much time he thought I had. He said to the doctor, "if you were a betting man and I said five years, you would say..." Dr Anwar shook his head, then Simon said "three years?" At this Dr Anwar held his hand out and made a kind of maybe sign. Even if he was doing it for my benefit, and this really only meant a year it lifted my spirits enormously.

Almost skipped out of that appointment, not sure Simon felt the same. He seemed even more confused and whilst we were having our meal with Mum and Norman he seemed irritable and agitated, especially when Norman referred to him being off work as "on his holidays". I thought Simon was going to explode.

Mum's birthday passed uneventfully, I think she is also confused and just wants me to do everything possible to live. It was a shame Lou and Jon couldn't have joined us but that night, although Lou was supposed to see Laura, she had to work until 11pm and Jon had to meet someone for my wacky baccy. Surprisingly, even my mother is on board with this, as it was her chiropodist that talked about it to her. Strange the way things work out.

Friday 16th May 2014

Simon went off to see Mandy to fill in insurance forms while I pottered about. Tina and Nigel had invited us round at 12.30 for a champagne afternoon tea with Sue and Paul. Nigel collected us and we had a wonderful afternoon, eating lovely sandwiches and cakes which Tina had made especially with us both in mind, i.e. no fat, watercress, quality Chicken and home-made scones. I couldn't resist the clotted cream though which I now realise has probably been my biggest downfall. I have always loved dairy.

Sadly, right at the end Jack's girlfriend (Jack being Sue's son) rang to say she had been made redundant from her job for lack of enthusiasm! Little did the company realise that they had cocked up and with Sue and Paul's help they wouldn't get off lightly.

Saturday 17th May 2014 - Holiday in Tenby

Lou hadn't come home so had to text us to ask if someone could collect her from Marc's at 10am. As Simon had to pop to his old office he said he would collect her. Unfortunately her phone had then died and she had fallen back to sleep. A not amused Simon rang me to say he had waited long enough and someone else would have to go and get her. A very apologetic Louise finally appeared, we then had a couple of tense hours trying to pack and leave the house.

Journey underway, we finally arrived at a beautiful cottage for the week and the sun was out. There was a little stream outside and comfy clean beds. After unpacking we wandered up to the little quayside pub for a drink, a little idyl, and before setting off back to the cottage Simon asked to buy a bottle of red wine. The guy said he couldn't do that but as he was staying local he would trust him to return another bottle for the one he gave us. Apparently Simon's Steve Hackett t-shirt had helped secure the deal. Simon was very chuffed with this.

That night while Louise cooked we tried the weed Jon had bought. I felt quite scared as I wasn't sure what effect it would have on me, as it turned out none. Simon, however, was on fire - his personality doubled, as he giggled his way through Louise's meatballs and I became very slightly irritated.

Sunday 18th May 2014

We had bought the juicer away with us and I had the best smoothie yet; apple, orange and kiwi, delicious. Really late start, eggs for breakfast then off to Tenby as the sun was shining and I was feeling good. We walked and paddled on the beach, took some lovely sunny day photos, walked up a big hill to see over the beach and rang Mum. Felt so well! Walked into town and had a drink and a laugh at a pub, nearly ate there but I didn't like a rusty rivet in a wall by us or the smell of disinfectant, so bought loads of stuff from a supermarket and headed back to the cottage. I had a second attempt at smoking and there was no real difference.

Monday 19th May 2014

In the morning we had gone to Carew Castle and Mill, felt really windy in my tummy and so tired. Every step was a bit of an effort, but I was determined I was going to do it. Afterwards we popped to the pub for a drink then set off for Saundersfoot. The weather was a bit changeable and I remembered I didn't really like the place the last time we came. Stopped for a drink but the pub had no atmosphere inside at all.

Set off for a coastal tour through a number of unattractive villages, but during this drive Simon found the place our holiday neighbour had recommended. It was picturesque, and the birthplace of Dylan Thomas. Beautiful little place, so we had a short walk finishing up a hill. Gosh, how out of condition I am, but managed it anyway. On the way back to the car we all needed a wee, so all of us crammed inside one of those automatic loos. What a laugh, smelly though.

Felt a bit sad in car journey back to the cottage. SO BLOODY UNFAIR.

Tuesday 20th May 2014

Woken up by rain and very grey skies, set off for Haverfordwest and after a few diversions because of the bloody rain ended up in Pembroke. Decided after a drink in another shitty pub with no atmosphere to go round Pembroke Castle. Not sure Simon was in the right mood, or Lou, whose cold had come out. The castle was quite good but had no instructions for route to take round it so we all got lost and split up and didn't really know the history of the place. By the time we had finished the sun was coming out finally and it was getting lovely and warm, we headed in the direction of a beach called Barafundle but ended up in a little Harbour just around the corner. I think it was the sort of place you walked to the beach while the tide was out then walked back via the cliffs. We just managed to scramble to the harbour and lie on the rocks for a bit, all of us fooling around, before setting off to find somewhere to eat.

After a sunny drink at one pub we stumbled across the Carew Inn where we had had a coffee a couple of days previous, I took the decision for us to eat there and we ate in a little room upstairs where I chose crab salad though unfortunately they were out of friggin' crab! Anyway upon hearing a guy choosing behind us, Lou and I opted for salmon, prawn and anchovy salad with new potatoes. It was scrummy but after only a small quantity I found I wasn't able to eat any more which was a real bugger as the salmon was delicious.

I quickly became quite uncomfortably full so once we had finished Jon and I walked out to the lake in front of the Inn, where the sun was warm on us, rang Nanny from the bridge by the lake and then set off for the cottage. We were going to stop again at the Cressley Arms at the quay, but I was so tired. Think the day had finally caught up with me and just wanted my bed.

Wednesday 21st May 2014
Had a very long lie in as still tired from the previous day. We were considering going mackerel fishing but the boats were either out or not going out again, one guy said he might do a trip at 2.30pm but considering it was 1.30pm a joint decision was made to head back to Tenby Beach, were we had a lovely few hours just relaxing, watching a Summer RNLI group of children playing games and learning life saving techniques. Had a chat with Lou and Jon about why they didn't think they were massively into sport, and about school and other things they had done, or how friends over the years

had upset them. Really lovely chat actually getting to know them. Afterwards we went to a fab bar on the beach and sat in the full sun people watching. Loved my Lambrusco which the kids had topped up with cider, but we were all getting a bit desperate for food now.

We all decided the best idea was to barbecue back at the cottage, which we did in our own little riverside garden. Lou and I prepared food whilst Simon and Jon set up camp. Oh what a feast we had. Lou cooked salmon and asparagus, followed by pork and salad, while we ate a starter of avocado. The food was cooked to perfection. One of the resident cats who was normally so well behaved suddenly turned into a predator and pestered us throughout the main course. Simon even had to carry him off and put him outside the gate to get rid of him. That didn't work either. Once we had finally got the pork and salad on our plates, with the cat tempted away by some salmon skin, he settled down. Although freezing cold and damp, it was the sort of magical evening where you laugh loads and realise how much you love one another.

Went in for a bath and a bit of a smoke, still not working much for me but made me a little squiffy and soporific. Had an early night.

Thursday 22nd May 2014
What a difference, the rain was horrendous. We weren't sure what to do but set off anyway towards Fishguard, then we planned to drop down to the coast to St Davids. Had such a laugh with my lovely family in the car, they are so ridiculous how they bounce off each other. Got out at St Davids

although still raining. Lou was frozen so we found a great pub and we were all starving, but they were not serving food. WTF! They had stopped until 6pm. So, we had a look around one of the towers that led to the cathedral. The kids found a stone relic with the word 'cunt' engraved on it, they found that hilarious. Set off for the car to look for somewhere to eat, don't think we will ever return to Wales, me especially; the pubs look like converted houses with no life and they shut at ridiculous hours and don't serve food, and even if they do it's expensive.

Arrived home knackered from the journey and as we were starving I suggested driving back to Wisemans Bridge which had a lovely sea view, the food looked nice and the wine was cheap, what could go wrong? Ordered some lovely food, a crab salad which was the most spectacular salad I'd ever seen, with blueberries, raspberries and apples etc. Simon decided on lamb shank but it was sold out so he went for lamb chops. Lou opted for chicken and ribs. The salads could not be faulted but Lou thought her sauce was slimy and Simon's chops were very well done. I filled up after about four mouthfuls and had pain in my side. Simon had a coughing fit, so between toilet visits it wasn't the best event to date. Lou and I left the boys to pay and we went back to the car. I was upset as the pain in my side was really bad, feels as though my spleen is so swollen that it stops me eating anything, feels worse than at the beginning of the week. Went back to the cottage, had a smoke in the bath and then we all watched "This Is Forty". Brilliant film, really enjoyed it. The kids and Simon as always were fantastic, encouraging me and telling me not to worry.

One of the nights during the holiday Louise couldn't sleep and came into our room. She had her hand up to her eyes and looked just like she did when she was a little girl. I went into her bed for a cuddle and to try and put her to sleep. We both had a little cry, so sad and however much we cry or do anything, it ain't gonna change a thing.

Friday 23rd May 2014
Packed for home, feel sad, journey took four and a half hours the traffic was terrible, tummy was really painful being doubled over in the car for so long, got very upset. Arrived home and Lou put me straight to bed while they all unpacked everything, so pleased to be in bed.

Saturday 24th May 2014
Pottered about in the morning, still feel weary. Mum and Norman came round, Mum said Auntie Gina had commented on how strong she was and Mum said it was though someone was helping her. Gina thought it was an angel that sits on all our shoulders, protecting and helping us. Mine must of been out when this shit hit the fan! Decided not to go to Denise and Pete's, didn't feel up to it as I had no energy and still had pain in my side. Cannot eat or drink, oh joy! Stayed in with Simon, smoked some weed and tried the Canabidoil.

Sunday 25th May 2014
Quiet day, prepared veg for later, went to B&Q and the Range, no one seems to sell nice flat sun beds anymore. Went to the park by Wyndley for a walk and saw a Greater Spotted Grebe, who kept on disappearing after diving. Had a lovely quiet lamb dinner with the kids and then watched the rest of the film "Blue Jasmine". Early to bed again.

Monday 26th May 2014
Sunny morning so set off again for a walk in the park, really busy, got agitated and took Simon off the main path onto a completely deserted pathway. What a difference, no bloody people! It was a bit embarrassing though when a guy in a wheelchair being pushed by his girlfriend overtook us!

The pain in my side is still uncomfortable so we went to Boots for some Gaviscon, then came home for a sleep. James rang, Simon's cousin, to say that his sister Louise and Hayden were splitting up. What a bloody shame did not see that coming. Helped Simon dust a bit and then rested for the remainder of the day. Still feel so weary.

How stupid is cancer. Simon remarked one day that it kills the very thing that keeps it alive. I wonder how many people document the pain of dying with cancer? I wouldn't think anyone would be advised to read this if they were in the same position. Well, I can tell you it's shit. I had felt great, taking hardly any painkillers at all, but since seeing the surgeon and going to Wales things are slowly changing. The pain in the side of my tummy hardly goes away and I can't tell if it's like hunger pains or really bad indigestion. But I think it is probably because the cancer is now in my spleen. I think it is swollen more now and is blocking the quantity of food I can eat, because I constantly feel full and bloated and as soon as I eat the pain in my side gets worse.

From taking only a couple of paracetamol each day, I now keep having to take ibuprofen and co-codamol, which I am trying to keep for night time as they make me sleepy. I feel like a fat old lady; I can't bend over properly since the operation and it has got increasingly worse. The only way I feel comfy is if someone rubs my side, like a baby to relieve wind, or if I wedge a cushion under the pain in my side. But the biggest relief is if I fall asleep.

Viv at St Giles said that slowly everything would shut down, and I think my tummy is doing that already. Who wouldn't choose a heart attack over this if they had the chance? This is preparing me for a big agonising finale and the only way to avoid the pain is to take the pain killers and morphine, and then, oblivion. Because I doubt my mind will give in. All I feel is anger at why we all have to suffer this. I suppose more indignities are to follow with no way out. What an absolute FUCKER!

Tuesday 27th May 2014

Woke feeling less weary so did some texts and paperwork. Popped out to see if we could find any nice sun beds. Obviously none were available for me at the moment. They all had horrible designs or were expensive and nasty. Will have to try elsewhere.

Off to Tesco next for some bits for Debbie, Tina, Sue and Denise, then home for a rest. By the time we got home I'd had enough euphoria for one morning, had well and truly waned and now felt tired and irritable. Had a lie down but my tummy pains just kept on niggling, even when the girls arrived I felt a bit out of it, like being the only sober person at a party. The food was crap, I burnt the first pizza then realised I had promised afternoon tea and dips and pizza wasn't quite the same, especially when Sue arrived later and I had no more pizza in the freezer.

The girls could see I was shuffling around and couldn't get comfy so they made me lie on the sofa and said I looked like Lady Godiva or similar with my arm over my head. Deb got fruit to put on me and took a photo. All this fun just made me really sad. I sat up and started to get weepy and the girls tried to comfort me but I just wanted Simon. They took me aside and Deb got upset, told me she would look after my mum for me.

Jon arrived home with special soap for my skin, and another to help with hair growth, which really upset Tina. It reminded her of her son, Jamie, and how shit cancer was and how all of this shouldn't be happening. By this time I had text Simon to come home, I really needed to go to bed and curtail the evening.

Everyone was on the drive way, the girls were all upset, I just wanted to go to bed. I felt upset firstly as tea had been crap, and then how uncomfortable I had been for the short time they had all been here. Not the best afternoon after what had been a promising start to the day.

Wednesday 28th May 2014

Had a lie in while Simon pottered about. Mum and Norman came after lunch which was quite pleasant. They were fairly upbeat and made me laugh and it was good having Simon around to keep everything positive. It was nothing like old times though. They only stayed a couple of hours and intimated they didn't see enough of us. Simon said it needed to be a bit more of a casual popping in than such an event maybe.

Thursday 29th May 2014

Couldn't sleep very well as still had pain and indigestion. Got Simon up at around 8.30am for a walk in the park, in the bloody rain again. I felt irritable but pleased we had gone.

We awoke to the drizzle, the pitter patter
Its relentless anodyne noise
Is only broken by the twisting movements of my love,
As she stirs hopefully against another day of pain.
This the Christ that butters our daily bread,
The choking realisation of loss and dread.

The working day begins for others
All those meaningful lives gather their thoughts
Against another monotonous day.
But now if someone could kiss and pass the key
We would both gladly return
And play Houdini against our now real world,
Lie silent and still, child like beneath normalities flag
unfurled.

The park was still, calm, awakening.
Captured within the rain of the day
The cows that grazed their way across our landscape
Recreate, imitate scenes of old England
Constable or Turner could brush this image, this view
We destined to enjoy, but to walk timeless and forgotten to
but a few.

The canopy of leaf, branch and tree, that we stroll beneath
Is drenched with tears from the skies,
We are secret now within the wood
She stretches out the anger within her body
As we tiptoe between unsound sod and solid ground,
The course of our lives now found

From somewhere between heaven and cloud
The birds drip their endless song, their chant.

The invisible noise of the air
I listen as I meander my hopeful dreamy way,
Caress the hand, the hand I have held so close for as long as I
need, recall
Each finger, each print and scar is intimate to me,
This ringed hand that set me free.

After our walk we went to Jenny's for a coffee which was nice, again I fidgeted throughout the visit, we came home and Valeria arrived with flowers, so I asked her in for a tea or coffee. Had a lovely hour with her, funny how some people's conversation seems more enlightening than others, she said she would like to come again.

Sorry, I've just remembered Wednesday evening was a bit of a disaster. Jon hadn't come home and as I was in pain Simon was trying to get the infuser for the weed working but it looked like it had broken - blood typical! So he's there trying to roll a spliff with not a clue, neither has Lou. In the end Jon appears to sort it all out. Simon had done well, but just not quite right. He rubbed some gel into my tummy then I smoked the spliff. Can you believe it, a 51year old woman smoking weed in her own bed?

I was already a bit squiffy from the co-codamol, but had two or three puffs and did start to drift a bit. For the first time that day I managed to turn my frown upside down. I said to Jon how I felt my face had forgotten how to smile. I giggled a little, then got upset, then went to sleep. The shortest high ever!

Two hours later, at about 9ish the door went, it was Karen Court looking right up at me as I peered out of the window. No one else had heard the door apparently! She was lovely, we invited her in and then Simon offered her a drink! Surprised he didn't invite her to dinner. There he is chatting away ten to the dozen and me sitting rocking in pain with a hoarse throat from smoking and a dazed expression, Anyway, after a while she left, and back off to bed I went, slightly irritated.

Thursday 29th May 2014 (earlier)
We went to the hospital, it was a quite clinic, saw a registrar which was good for a change. She explained the pain after chemo can be caused because it upsets your gastric balance, but also the cancer may be close to nerve endings, causing more pain. She gave me oramorph and advised just to take co-codamol regularly and that I must try to open my bowels daily. She also gave us the hormone therapy pills, which again she said would make me put on weight. I don't know how, as I can hardly force anything down me now. Saw Mr Bolega briefly, then came home, Simon ran round getting prescriptions while I helped prepare dinner for him. I think my stomach is so confined, it doesn't know what to expect next.

Friday 30th May 2014

Ok-ish night's sleep, still woke up but managed to go back off. I feel a bit brighter, checking Facebook and writing my journal is always a good sign.

Sarah and Lynne due to pop in later, Simon was just tidying up whilst I rolled around in bed trying to alleviate the pain. There are not so many tears now on a daily basis, just an acceptance of the way things are. Simon and I hardly touch upon the subject unless we have to. That's probably more me shutting the cancer out than him, as we both know we still have lots of paperwork to complete.

Only Sarah could make it in the end. It's always a delight, she is so trendy and well turned out, doesn't look much over forty, let alone fifty. She had made me a lemon drizzle cake but was a little upset when she found out I couldn't eat it... judging by the portions Simon was handing out it would soon be gone anyway. I had a lovely time with her, but was knackered by the time she had gone. Went up to bed for a rest on the proviso that Simon would either leave me there or pop in just before Louise and James, Simon's cousins, were leaving. I slept quite well and then could hear James say, "well we must be making a move", so I threw myself together to go and have a quick chat, as poor Louise is going through her own hell. Quickly caught up, then they left. So glad I got to see them.

Why do we not remember or think of family, until it could be
too late?
I have left my family, my kindred spirits
Hoping they would survive on their own personal waves of
fate.
The bundle of souls held within, close and distant households
Are and have always been known to me.
I ignored them in a selfish belief, that I was setting them free,

I was second to the tape
When my wife unknowingly planned her tragic escape
But my kith and kin without reservation
Held us all so close within
In each self-beating heart, slowly each day, torn slothfully
apart.

Saturday 31st May 2014
Another rubbish day, it poured with rain all day. I didn't feel
great. It's been a quite uneventful, constipated day. Felt guilty
that I needed to see Mum more.

Sunday1st June 2014
Cancelled Kathy until after our holiday. But we had woken to
the sun and I wanted to go to the Sutton Fun Run so Simon
nipped out earlier to check the site and one of the traffic guys
controlling the roads said he would allow us through to park
a lot closer, as I could not walk all the way in this year.

Felt slightly conspicuous as I decided to wear a head scarf, but set off with chairs and bottled water in hand. Fortunately this year we didn't meet lots of people on the side of the road that we knew, but we saw everyone that we knew that was running; Louise, Ella, Anne Beaumont, Pam, Debbie Horton and Lauren. They're all very brave I must say as it was pretty hot even at 11.30am.

Came home and called Mum to come down to see us sooner. I feel she needs to see me more, but for less formal visits, just to pop in have a coffee and then go. I think they want it to be some sort of formal visit, with us sitting and having intense conversation, but it is always the same subject.

CANCER: LOOKING ON THE BRIGHT SIDE
No need to pluck, chin, moustache and eyebrows daily.
Save on hair cuts.
Time saved styling and blow drying hair.
Lie ins.
No work.
Get to see more of family and friends.
Free prescriptions.
Beautiful flowers and messages from friends and colleagues who you didn't know thought so much of you.
Get to talk about you all the time (tedious).
Pensions and insurances all pay out early.
Simon gets to be at home all the time.
Hairs have all dropped out of my nose.

Monday 2nd June 2014
Had an appointment with Dr Gupta at Good Hope Hospital to sort my head out, told him how angry I was, and that that

would never change, and how I had always been such a positive person. He tried to show me a number of meditation and self-help clips on his computer, but they wouldn't open and he was quite happy for me to have a few clicks, but to no avail. Although I had been to the toilet early that morning and was expecting to be on top of the world, my tummy was still painfully grumbling away. I found it hard to concentrate on what he was saying. He was a lovely gentleman, but I'm not sure he had the same brilliant effect on me. They all give you time to talk about yourself, but I could do that forever and then I get bored while they explain the why and wherefores. I think I've officially seen enough counsellors to date!

Mum came in the afternoon while the St Giles Nurse was here which gave them something to listen to, and I didn't have to entertain them. Soon after they had gone, although I felt mentally tired, I needed a walk and for once the park was perfect; the right temperature, the right number of dogs, people and cars. A good walk.

Tuesday 3rd June 2014
I'm still having constipation problems so am taking a regular strong laxative. I rested briefly in the morning, then popped out to sign our wills with Simon. I felt quiet and walked like an ill person.

A district nurse called Yvonne called to see us all and Jon and Simon met and entertained her until I came down from the bedroom. She was a nice lady.

Sue and Dawn were due to pop in briefly, I was a bit sick before they arrived and thought I'd have to cancel them, but settled after a rest. We had a lovely couple of hours catching up and it was great to hear all the in house gossip. Simon brought Brian back from the pub and I briefly chatted with him, but at the back of my mind this whole constipation thing is terrifying me. I feel so incredibly bloated, cannot bend properly or bear clothes pushing on my tummy. I made my excuses and Jon took me off to bed. The problem is if I don't eat, there won't be much to come away, anyway. I feel this massive tumour is squashing everything.

Wednesday 4th June 2014

Great morning with Simon, we set off to the Fort late by the time we'd faffed around. Bought an orange maxi dress for our holiday plus a hat which Simon found, and mascara. Took a couple of things back to T.K.maxx and that was me done for the day.

Exhausted again! The funny thing was I needed to eat while we were out so we went to M&S and Simon suggested the trio of fish sandwiches, bearing in mind he doesn't like fish. I know he would do anything for me, anyway I think I am slowly converting him. Rested pretty much for the remainder of the day. The nights are not good for pain, I'm uncomfortable from around 11pm to 5am each night, and this whole constipation thing makes me think it could be the end because nothing seems to be able to move further than my chest area.

Thursday 5th June 2014

Simon set off early to take Mum and Norman to the city hospital for Norman's scan. They were in and out pretty quickly and all in good spirits. I, on the other hand, finally had a poo! You cannot appreciate what a relief that was. I felt as though I was completely blocked from top to bottom, not even any fluids wanted to go through but strangely, something must have worked. The relief made me really upset as I shared this with Lou, then Mum and Norman. I still don't think mum comprehends what is going on as she keeps asking why I am like this or like that - well I don't bloody know! I decided to cancel Amanda in the afternoon as not feeling up to so many visitors anymore.

Friday 6th June 2014 (BAD MOOD TODAY SO, SORRY ALL)

Ridiculously overbooked myself today, but if people only stayed for around an hour it wouldn't be so bad. Debbie and Nicky came in the morning which was lovely, bearing more flowers and kind words, telling me how short staffed they were while they wasted two hours lapping up the sun in my garden. I don't think they had any intention of running back. I really needed them to have left after an hour. Not long after Lisa arrived bearing cake and more kind words, how much like Helen she is.

I did feel a bit out of it as she and Simon chatted about old times, the cancer and all the tablets seem to be slowly robbing me of my personality. I am so tired most of the time and the rest of it I just cannot be bothered covering the same old ground over and over again. Lisa said she would take Simon out for a drink one afternoon while Lou was around to take care of me. Well there is no way that is going to happen while I am still here. I think he would rather be with me than some other woman. Take your own husband out Lisa!

Due to go to Sue and Paul's in the evening and after a sleep I felt a bit more up for it, in fact although we were only there around two to three hours I enjoyed the conversation and dry roasted peanuts, but sadly not Paul's Peach Cava. Grace and her new boyfriend were there too and she had just landed a job, so all around a really chilled night where everyone could talk without one person taking over, thank you Sue and Paul xxx.

Saturday 7th June 2014
Sue and Steve came to see us, Sue bought some flowers and we had a good catch up with a few tears. The boys briefly popped down the road but Simon only had one pint, think this rash on his body has scared him and he didn't drink anymore that weekend I don't think.

Sunday 8th June 2014
Simon didn't feel too good but I had promised to see Rhianne as she was back from Italy, so we arrived at about 11.30am, Denise was lovely and specifically asked how I was. They're all excited about their possible house sale, so good chat all round. Chilled for the rest of the day.

Monday 9th & Tuesday 10th June 2014
Spent some time getting ready for the holiday to Port d' Andratx, Majorca. Well actually Lou and Simon did it all really, I had felt pretty crap for two days and was particularly

horrible to Mum and Norman on Monday when they were only trying to help. But honestly, who spends twenty minutes folding the washing out of the washing machine BEFORE hanging it on the line? This comes from having too much time on your hands.

I did feel awful though, as the look on my face must have said it all. Then I bossed Mum into driving her car to the shops at Princess Alice as Norman's driving scares me. I forgot that she is an old lady now, struggling with her seat belt as she's wearing too many layers of clothes. She said to me in Tesco, "Norman does try his best". How bad did I feel?

Felt guilty after they had gone, they are only trying their hardest but all this worry is making Mum's mind worse I think. Cancelled my nails for Tuesday as felt too crap to go, Lou sorted my feet out though.

Wednesday 11th June 2014
Problem free escape from home, most unusual but all quite chilled. Still wish I had a bit more energy though. Checked bags in then picked up wheelchair. This was an ordeal although I am glad we organised it. It was not a conventional wheelchair and it was difficult to manoeuvre and although Simon was trying his best he got a bit agitated. Firstly we couldn't find the lift and then he kept banging my legs off various posts and pillars. Anyway, once seated I felt quite happy.

Good flight with no problems, thank goodness, and the same at Palma Airport except that we had to wait a long time to pick up the hire car (even with a wheelchair). Got to the car park and felt sick, thought I was going to have a major accident but once the journey was underway and the air-con was on I relaxed.

Could not have been treated better by my family, put me to bed while they unpacked then we chilled by the pool and I stayed up into the evening. My first little dip in the pool made me cry, didn't think I would get here as I felt so poorly over the last few weeks. So to stretch out in the crystal clear pool with the palm trees overhead was quite a high point.

Shall I pray to him now,
Now that I am 20,000 feet closer to his ear?
Will he hear me now, my hopes gleaming above these clouds
Not darkened by the dull skies of earth?
Free thought, free feelings, new optimism, as we soar above
this world
On wings of lifetime memories, and loose change family
things.

She sleeps when once the sun would make her fidget with
excitement,
Its draw, its glow of enticement
Of lazy days, of early evening sunshine, of food and wine,
The unbreakable bond of a family church.
But her eyes struggle to capture the past
To continue the ubiquitous, relentless restaurant search.

Do you hear me then, up there in your atmosphere?
Thin air like your belief in us
To treat carefree loving souls thus
Is to forget our very earthly names and existence
Our cloudless vision of being alive

To navigate a ripple free path through your sacred, scaring
life
We were happy to carry our baggage, to the end of your
realm
But to unpack our private contents in front of all,
Have it picked over, each weakness exposed, each strength
examined

The suitcase of our lives slowly emptied,
Its contents discarded on the busy runway of every day.
Our passport to happiness withdrawn, revoked.
Each blank face now hides a tear, hides a dark thought of
anger
Sleeping but vigilant in its eagerness to be provoked.

So at 20,000 feet you turned away,
The sun was beautiful, the sun was fire.
But you dispatched a personal Judas to stab our backs.
And so when she has gone to you forever
We shall not pray to you, or worship you,
Or keep your boarding pass of restraint
To everyone and no one, please take care, for we now have
nothing to declare.

Thursday 12th June 2014
Got up late as I was weary from the journey. I had a wonderful relaxing day by the pool and another rest. Lou did my makeup on the bed for me and then they drove me into town where Si and I stopped in a bar people watching and the kids went off to find a restaurant. They told us the prices are all about the same, how gullible we are! Anyway, we went to an Italian restaurant close by and I shared a tiny bit of their meals. Simon had a beautiful sea bass, Lou had prawn linguine and Jon had salmon ravioli. Lovely food but they were tiny portions for the boys. The little I had stayed down but I couldn't face Jon's ravioli. Afterwards they were all so good, holding my hand, checking if I was okay then, inevitably, getting me back into bed since I'm always knackered now.

Friday 13th June 2014
I felt okay when I woke up except for a pain in my calf muscle, so Simon and I drove down to the port and walked around it, and then up towards the town. I sat on a bench and Simon went to get me a refreshing drink, or so I thought. He took an age so I rang mum. Cannot say how disappointed I was when he returned with a limited edition green tea drink – he just doesn't seem to get it, I don't like tea!

Felt a bit ratty as I walked towards the car, as I was so thirsty and just fancied a can of Sprite or something similar. When there is so little you actually fancy, little things like this become such a major issue. Sorry Si if I was grumpy xxx.

Chilled around the pool for the afternoon then set off for St Elm for a change of scene. The best part for me was the toasted ham, cheese, tomato and onion sandwich, which hit the spot in every way. Felt so relaxed, my tummy wasn't playing up for once. We then sat on the beach for an hour or so which was good while they had a swim. I was too tired to be bothered to walk over the shale and didn't want to lose my hat in the wind. On leaving St Elm I was completely worn out but did sit out, back at the apartment, whilst Simon and the kids prepared a BBQ. This is Louise's forte normally but in fact this time the boys cooked the meat.

The ridiculous thing was the minute we sat down I looked at the tiny bit of food on my plate and I couldn't bear the thought of eating any of it. Managed a slice of avocado and a bit of mozzarella and that was my lot. It's so strange, almost like a mental block now.

Saturday 14th June 2014
Had a really bad night I was up and down with wind pain, wanting to go to the loo but unable to get the pain under control. By the morning I felt even worse, so decided to stay at home while Simon and the kids set off for the beach. I'm so glad they went as it makes me more relaxed and I know they enjoyed the change of scene, even though none of them cared much for the beach.

While they were out I slept, managed to eat a tiny bit and then actually got out in the sun, firstly in the little garden of the apartment, and then by the pool. I also managed to catch up with my diary and took another look at the book Simon had bought me. I don't mind my own company at all and Si and the kids must understand this, which I think they are doing now, thankfully. After another short sleep we got ready to eat in town.

Everything seemed right, I'd rested, time was perfect, Lou had made me look beautiful again and I felt really nice. I just had this niggling tummy pain which I hoped would disappear soon when the tablets kicked in. Sadly this wasn't to be and as I grimaced through a jug of Sangria, in a perfect spot overlooking the bay, the pain didn't subside. And we were still due to eat. I felt as though all I needed was a huge fart to clear my system.

I found a lovely restaurant which was brilliant value for money, situated up a side street, but with perfect views of the harbour. The table and chairs were at a sixty degree angle and however we moved our seats it felt as though we were sliding downhill. But hey ho, not moving now.

Unfortunately the food was then very delayed, which under normal circumstances would not have been a problem, but everyone became agitated worrying about my pain and the time to get the meals. I've never seen Louise devour so many cigarettes so quickly. Such a shame really as when the food came it looked stunning. It was everything I would have chosen - Louise's especially. She had mussels, squid, fish and prawns, it was just my kind of meal but I couldn't even manage a morsel. It's so strange, is this signal coming from my brain or my stomach? I felt so awful as I had ruined a beautiful evening, even if I hadn't eaten, just because I couldn't sort the tummy pain and couldn't even take the second lot of co-codamol.

Simon, my knight in shining armour, still managed to drive us home safely and after a short lie on the settee I retired to my little blue and lemon bedroom again. This was not what I had planned for the week at all.

Awaken to our yesterday
I roll over and see her as before,
All locks and curls tumbling around that face,
The face of my life.
Eyes closed in deep, restful repose.
What dreams lie behind those shuttered eyes?
What plans she draws, with raised arms in sleep
Her fingers trace an imaginary course across each arm.

She sleeps with the sun beneath her pillow
I learnt, if I lay, so close, so still, I could feel the heat,
The light stirring dreams, that would escape when she
moved,
Seep across the sheets, pulling me, wrapping me in.
I was never allowed to know where she had been,
But somehow in real time I knew, we would be standing
there
I, so happy to live in this sunshine world,
Where even the daily routine of care was filled
With future foreign lands, random wonderful plans.

But now we lounge under the same sun
With all future plans once so vibrant and sparkling
Tethered now to this earthly ailment,
Caught in a cruel web, so neatly spun.
We no longer have those restless airport heels,
Now fettered and tied
Understanding a life that tricked us, it lied.

Her body writhing for a second release,
To be as we were before,
All shining eyes and freedom footprints, in late afternoon sun

Sunday 15th June 2014

Father's Day. I didn't even remember to wish it to Simon when he came in the lounge to find me after I'd tried to escape his snoring. Feel oh so selfish all the time. Went back to bed then had chronic wind pain and felt sick again, so Si found me a bucket and there I am, in all my glory, throwing up and going to the loo at the same time.

Decided just to take the oramorph as cannot bear to take tablets anymore, and the oramorph seems a quicker pain fix. I took myself back off to bed again until around 3.30pm. It's a shame really as the weather was not so good and I think they'd have been better if they could have sunbathed. But, they set off to the town to try and find a nutrition drink for me, to shop, and have a couple of beers.

I think they were okay, but know they missed me. I did feel slightly better when they got back, so after a prolonged attempt at freshening up I finally made it in to the garden to enjoy the last of the day's sun with the four of us all together.

While I am writing, Lou and Jon are preparing a Father's day meal for Simon, which I am sure will be lovely. The last two nights have probably been the worst since this journey began. I seem to have overcome the tears and blanked out the pain when I can, so I don't have to cry very often, but now there is a numbness, even a coldness about me. I have built a little shell around me. It feels like a bit of a protection. I find it hard to believe that no one seems to want to listen to my whole story, and now, how could we move forward in any way? Everything is just about pain relief and so far nothing they have given me has, in my opinion, hit the spot at all. One hole patched immediately leads to another gap somewhere else which needs sorting. I am not getting a single day of relief from the misery of either wind, tummy pain, or this huge growth I seem to be carrying around with me. One tablet will make me sleepy but within an hour I'm awake again and still in pain. I am finding even taking the tablets a trial as I just want to throw up.

7.15pm, Sunday evening
Actually lying writing this journal and feeling okay, although whatever chair or position I sit in I feel uncomfortable, but I am not griping with pain. Around me the water sprinklers feed the garden and a few children play quietly in the distance. The temperature is still warm, although I could do with a blanket. However in comparison to some of the last forty eight hours, I feel relatively comfortable.

If the doctors and hospital cannot help me maintain a reasonable level of comfort then quite frankly I can't see the point with continuing treatment. I may as well just be asleep all the time, because if every moment is taken with thinking about which tablet to take next, to control which pain, then surely for all of us death would be a better option?

Reality check, hair still not growing back but Jon reckons I have a lovely beard coming on.

Monday 16th June 2014
Got up at an okay sort of time and eventually managed to drag myself outside into the sun. I feel crap again. I've had no food since a slice of pizza yesterday, and I bought that up on our way back to the apartment with Simon after getting all

dressed up to go out in the evening. I wonder if I will ever get to wear these clothes again, or who Simon will pass them on to? Maybe Louise, but that would probably be too upsetting for her, and too old fashioned.

After Simon had settled me down, he walked back down to meet the kids. They had a lovely meal, Simon had lamb shoulder with the inevitable two tiny potatoes, Lou had fish wrapped and stuffed with prawns, and Jon had a lobster claw with prawns and tagliatelle. This last one is probably one of my all time most favourite things again, and I currently couldn't even get it past my lips. Is it all in my head? I dozed while they were away and then on in to the night. Fortunately I had no more chronic wind pain.

We three now lie within this trench
In fear of what lies above, of death of love,
The entrails of our lives strewn across the earth, the blood
stained mud.
Why are we unable to hold back this tide, to breathe above
this flood?
The open expanse of this oncoming wilderness
Peppered only with barbed wire memories
That cling to parental metal, like child with outstretched
hand.

She who each day wakes
To the repetitive pain, that drags her from half sleep to
another day
With the dread of new unforgiving symptoms
That steal and drown her smile, her personality,
Darkening her every dawn.
Her suffering is now
Ours, ours is yet to be born.

But now although we three tremble with unspoken thoughts
and lost glances
As we shake deep and dark within this current furrow,
We still have her waking eye and daily I see
How beautiful the love of a son with such an open heart,
And how distressing the love of a daughter as the anger tears
her apart.

We rally forth, collect yesterday's memories, encase them
with today's.
Our strength is her need, our eclipsed hearts are shamed
By her still beating lust for life
Our open road of fear, met by her dream to walk beside us
arm in arm,
Frenzied desire for that golden view,

Entranced and captured, we slouch towards a close
Walking backwards away from sunlight
And forward into remembered rainbows.
Alberabello candlelight
Aegean sunsets on once invincible, unsinkable lives.
We shall return again, steadfast in yearning
For horizons of cherished Pollyanna skylines.

Tuesday 17th June 2014
Final day of the holiday, was this such a great idea? I have
not been well since we arrived. Have had no energy
whatsoever and my appetite has been crap to the point of
hardly eating a thing. The apartment has been amazing
though, better than home for comfort. To have the warm sun
on your back, to hardly wear any clothes and to not have to
worry about my makeup and wig all the time has been
incredible. Simon, Lou and Jon could not have been more
attentive, but without pushing me to do anything I knew I
couldn't do. They have left me alone when I have needed my
own space.

I wonder if I will ever return here? I don't think so really. I
would love to come back in a few weeks. All the things we
take for granted; I keep thinking about the walk in the port

and seeing the huge fish swimming under the ducks in the harbour, the shimmer of the sun on the boats in the port, and actually being able to take each element in, to remember it when you get home, the foggy mountains and rocks in the background, just like the place I wanted to take Simon to meet Chris Stewart from Genesis. Sweet dreams no longer to become reality, robbed by fucking cancer.

Parched earth of this sunlit isle,
Its mountains scattered with happy homes
That gleam, shine in the evening light
When you return to a long missed place
And know in some way you are home.
The broken pieces strangely seem to fit.

We travel abroad to rediscover our past,
Rekindle her smile, her desire for heat, succulent and absorbing.
There was summer and there was always you.
Rejoice in soles burnt on golden sands,
Recline a body to shed the accumulated waste of another year,
Feel it drip, evaporate as your salt drenched fingers
Dry, in clear blue skies.

The heat blinds your eyes
But refills your soul, makes you whole.
This time waters drain freely from this cracked family vessel
So the spirit is not replacing itself as it should
And we are receiving the taster menu of what is to be.
As our guiding light, our beacon
Wrestles with the demons and the ills within her body.

So reluctantly she abandons her flock,
Virgin paths for a father and his children
In search of new bonds to pull us through.
Ironic that we purchase trinkets and charms
For when we return to you.

This place is an altar of some strange release,
This harbour with its shifting light upon captured waves
Where on fashionable nights the people promenade,
Chic and shallow, deep and hollow,
Parade their labelled life under this turning heat.
Its fading warmth pulls them, ties them together,
Like moths they are drawn but are gone forever.

Watching who's looking, looking who's watching,
We embrace and enjoy this wealthy human procession,
This cavalcade of life serenades our eyes.
We are but guests to your streets
We are simply passing through
We shall leave no mark or memory
Of our return to you.

The moon shines a smile
And lights the myriad homes and souls of your heaven.
We shall vanish, return north
To fight the battle we bought to your shores.
We shall endure until all is lost
And only then when your sun rises
On this, your enchanted coast, and ours quietly sets,
Shall we count the coins and weigh the cost.

Wednesday 18th June 2014

Needless to say I went to bed with a tight bloated tummy which worried me because of possible pain on the plane. Thankfully Simon had adjusted getting up times to allow for hiccups and difficulty in getting to the airport on time. I couldn't do a thing but the three of them cleaned and sorted it all, no problem and no fall outs.

Set off in pain and upon arrival at the airport I knew I needed a wheelchair as I could hardly walk and was afraid I might have an accident. It was a really tense twenty minutes spent near the toilets and finding a wheelchair. God was I relieved when Jon and Simon showed up with a chair to push me to the check in desk. Unfortunately after they had checked Simon and I in the kids had to go the normal route, so the system rather abandoned Simon and I and he had to push me and drag a suitcase. Poor bloke, will be dead before me at this rate. He is so amazing, my one in a million, I'm sure he would do absolutely anything for me if I asked.

The flight was delayed for an hour and unloading at the other end took an age, but once we were in the taxi I felt I could relax a little and virtually collapsed in bed until later on that evening.

Thursday 19th June 2014

Didn't sleep great but felt safe and closer to help. That day we saw the badger doctor, not an actual doctor for badgers, but an out of hours doctor in case anyone was wondering, Jessica haha! He said my problem was constipation and that I was completely blocked and they would need to keep everything really fluid down there. A couple of other nurses came too with other notes and advice. Simon set off for the medicine whilst I awaited further instructions, all the info was good and I started to believe a little more in what they were telling me.

My problem is I don't feel it's constipation, but that I have just grown a complete blockage and all their laxatives won't work anyway.

Friday 20th June 2014

Still feel shit, on the advice of the district nurse I decided to call the doctor in rather than try to get an appointment. The doctor dutifully arrived around 11.30am, she was excellent, I won't go into too much detail but as an experienced doctor she sorted out all my tablets, sheets and medication for me, which was all ready to collect later. I'm very pleased with the Hawthorns Surgery.

I had not seen mum since we got back, so she came round and we sat upstairs with the district nurse and she asked me a few questions. Mum did comment that they did seem to just look at you, but she didn't know I had spoken to them in some detail over the previous two days.

It was lovely to see Mum, I felt I had been grumpy on previous visits and it's not her fault. I just want to cuddle up to her in bed and make it alright.

I was told to virtually triple up on my laxatives, and they did work! Had a pleasant afternoon with them though a little short as is the norm now. When they left I went to bed which is pretty much where I stayed all afternoon, poor Simon was backwards and forwards getting prescriptions; he was trying so hard for me to make sure that I'd got stronger injections in the house if necessary over the weekend.

Saturday 21st June & Sunday 22nd June 2014
Haven't ever felt so poorly as this before in my life. I'm not sleeping as the griping pain is almost continuous in my tummy, so I can't lie on one side or the other. Morphine keeps making me all jerky and then I wake up and chat shit. My tongue is really dry and then sore and the pain from not eating is making me crabby.

Think Simon would magic me something to eat if he thought I would enjoy it but to no avail, everything I put in my mouth is either too salty, sweet, powdery or uncomfortable. One symptom seems to calm then another will start, that's why I feel such a pain with the kids who think I must be making it all up!

The weather is beautiful and everyone is gaily going about their business enjoying the sun and I haven't even left the house since touch down on Wednesday. I have seen my Mum but find this even more sad at times, we just cover the same ground over and over again; she has nothing but cancer to talk about, understandably, but I still promise to ask the Doctors the appropriate questions for her. Unfortunately she seems to be the one getting the kicking from all sides, I don't know why, but firstly repeating herself over and over again to Norman as I give up after the first two attempts. I need to back off as all of her suggestions are valid, just further down the state of play. Simon and Jon are probably the most civil towards her as they have always been much softer and kinder.

Monday 23rd June 2014

I can't even write properly now! As Lou was off work we decided we needed to go out somewhere together, so after taking hours to get ready headed up towards Lichfield/Stafford. At our initial stop at Wolsey Bridge Garden Centre, my tummy was really sore, almost exactly the same as the visit here after being discharged from hospital in March. I left Lou to have a look around as we decided we would need a wheelchair. Once settled in we had a quick look but all of it was still really expensive and there were no sun beds which I probably would have paid extra for, but £200 for one beige bed!

Ended up at Blithfield Reservoir and had an ice cream, quite nice but everything I eat never tastes how it should. Once we got home, Mum and Norman popped in. I do keep telling them how we got on and what we had been up to but my mind finds it hard to take it in and of course one day turns into the next then the next. While they were here my hearing had been playing up as though I had just got off a plane, but after a time it cleared itself, thank goodness, and we did manage to have a bit of a laugh in the garden.

Tuesday 24th June 2014

I was awake on and off as usual all night, at about five or six I decided to make notes for Viv from St Giles as today was the first time we had seen her since the holiday. I wrote down the meds that need changing to ask her opinion about going to London for this trial.

Pottered around, had a bath and dozed until she arrived. She's a nice lady but so laid back, I think she could see we were upset and annoyed though with the way the treatment was working out, i.e. not very well! She is going to refer me to the St Giles Hospice for treatment and respite to see if they can get everything sorted as we feel there are too many toes in the broth at the moment.

During our chat my tummy had got increasingly worse again with this period back pain. Once she had left and after another little chat together, and also after a lot of back rubbing, we thought that we get out anyway as it was such a lovely day and it would be quiet. So we set off for Chasewater but my pain seemed to be getting worse and we couldn't find a nice cool spot to park or sit. So after much fidgeting and moaning we set off for home via Four Oaks.

I rang Viv and Yvonne, the district nurse. Lou was at home. I was in bed. I'd had a gorgonzola cracker, dozed, then did some notes to help me finish off the day as I'm so bloody tired.

Wednesday 25th June 2014
Again, woke feeling pretty crap, no respite from this pain as I take in more pain killers on top of movicol and pessaries. In a low mood although I did feel more up to seeing Mum and Norman, as each time before I seem to be taking my anger and frustration out on them.

Mum was very low as she is not sleeping well. I think she wants to talk to us about more important matters that she maybe doesn't want to talk to Norman about anymore.

I had a pleasant afternoon with them, Simon popped to his old office where I think he got a bit upset, Lou sat with us for a bit but it was Norman who suggested going home as he was hungry. I was more than happy to go to bed. Chatted in the evening with Simon for a bit about funerals and the kids, once I was in bed I was okay, but I still have this continuous period/labour type pains.

I glanced at the papers today
And it appears I have vanished, gone far away
Lost within the pages of that social class paper for the
people.
This assertive, self gratifying local ink stained rag,

How easily the wheels of business need to crush a past
I cannot, must not blame their tread mill of thought.
The valuer is dead, long live the valuer.
The small watermark I left
Will bleed within the relentless tides of trade

This yearning, this desire for the wealth and way
Will blind some, 'til your loved ones are lost,
Dead, speechless, torn hearts turned away.

I am erased purged from sight, it is a matter of fact
And I cannot blame their lack of tact
To move their wheel their lonely stone
Their belief in routine and the mundane is right
Set against our small lives of weekend freedom
Forgetting profit for living
That balance sheet to our drunken fight.

They have been good to me
But my fractured life will always release the bitter kernel
With all its poison and regret
So I write with such weak defiance
Against the love I feel for those who cut me loose
They have given all they could
Set against my frail thoughts and weakness
Supported and stabilised, by their ever giving Maypole dance
around my life.

I do not blame them
I blame my seemingly ever decreasing life
The circles I dance, those tightening ribbons
That restrict my daily view
Have ingrained in me an embittered
Darkened eye of life to look through.

At around 1am. I didn't know what to take for the best,
paracetamol hardly touches the pain and oramorph lasts
around and hour and just makes me drop off then jerk awake,
so I took some co-codamol, heaved and got to the bathroom
where I threw up on the floor. I'm not sure I can carry on like
this for much longer, I would rather be dead.
After Simon had cleared up he decided to ring the badger
doctors again.Then ensued one of the longest day's ever.

Thursday 26th June 2014
The badger doctors, I must say, have all been pretty amazing
and after lots of phone calls and examinations the doctor said
that Good Hope Hospital wanted to admit me. After climbing
into the ambulance with a couple of buffoons who took all
my OBS again and explained reasons for this and that to the
nth degree, we finally set off. It would have been quicker to
drive there, but we did go straight up on to a ward which was
just awakening. I've never seen Good Hope so quiet.
I had more checks then more OPS and a very strange
question from the Doctor, "did we live in a house?" Was this
a fucking joke?! He then wanted to take bloods and all the

veins he tried to tap into had been affected by the chemo, which I had told him before he started. At this point I flipped and said no, I wanted to go home and that we were being pushed from pillar to post with no one taking specific control of our care.

The doctor realised we both meant business and got one of his more experienced colleagues to see me, who was far more supportive and listened to us both. Between us we caused a bit of a stir, Simon went to see Dr Anwar and Vanessa to push for some action. I think Dr Anwar and Mr Bolega had conversations, then a senior Nurse saw us and sorted out a plan, then I even got to see Dr Chapman who is a surgeon, for his opinion.

Had a strong enema which did work then an x-ray and an ultrasound scan. There are some fantastic individuals who are working in the NHS for all the right reasons. Ultrasound did show pockets of fluid which may be able to be drained, but there were no promises. The staff on wards 2 and 17 treated us like kings and with respect which was obviously reciprocated. The registrar came to chat to us at around 5-6pm to discuss our whole journey to date. He has been the only one who has listened to our story in full. His aim is to try and fit a drain to remove the fluid, which in future may need doing again but at least it is with a view to a life of some description.

I could have hugged that young man to death; a shiny star in a sea of blackness which consisted of pain management which just wasn't working, like the packets of bloody movicol, when had I jumped on the escalator of doom.

After such a long day, this evening is a bit of an anti-climax, the calm before the storm as the next few days and nights will show.

Sitting her in a private room with huge picture windows, I plan to relax shortly and try to absorb all the shit from the last two to three weeks. I am now officially going to rest.

Friday 27th June & Sunday 28th June 2014

Everyone went home thinking all was sorted, the drain was in and the pain seemed under control   At around 4.30am I started to feel really sick and had diarrhoea. I called one of the nurses who said she would be right with me, the indignity of needing the loo and being sick was awful, I couldn't easily get to the phone but saw five missed calls from Simon and then he rang again and I was just about able to slide over and answer the call to tell him to come ASAP, as I felt so ill.

He arrived and I continued to be sick half hourly for the next twelve hours - it was yellow, green, black and so acidic that it made my lip bleed. In between being sick I had to use the commode in the bedroom with Simon's help. I don't even know how he even managed to stay in that room with me.

After a bit of a slow start the nurses seemed to realise just how poorly I was, then I became surrounded by doctors and all sorts trying to control the sickness. In the end I had to have a driver fitted which was the only thing with the right drugs to stop me being sick. My real concern is that when I am at the end stage, who is going to stop the pain and sickness and put me to sleep? I think even Simon was worried as he commented to Helen that he thought he was losing me. Cancelled all visitors Saturday as too poorly.

All the flippant wonder of being the wounded soul
Is lost as I watch you, your body race in oramorph sleep,
Sleep fall to wide awake
Break your slumber, never to allow a moments rest, for peace
To put a mind asunder.

Those bright eyes roll now to a heaven inside your head,
Your lips move in mysterious conversation
With the living and the dead.
Still I sit and watch the one I love,
This tangible closeness, this distant hurt separates us
As you struggle to negotiate calm and painless rest
With those voices that move your lips
And manipulate your morphine world

I left you calm on oncology ward two,
The fluid leaving, relieving you
Realigning your body so swelled and spent
The protective bubble of your cancer now burst
Its life force draining its life force starved,
Hopefully slowing its relentless thirst.

What disease kills the host it feeds off
In blind desire to control the whole?
Like dictators and their empires, destroying the free, the
beating heart
'Til no pulse is found in all who serve.
Comfort in death, in the unknown
For it has grown more appealing than the now.

This battle is fought in home, hospice and hospital
With each manoeuvre of the disease
Pitted against us, our surgeons, our medical physicians
Who try and second guess a body's decisions.

Her twenty four hour battle has begun
As we fight for the ground that we had won,
The spewing armies of suffering, wretched and tore at my
love's heart,
The heaving body
Comforted only by an innocent hope that care will endure,
Will hold back the gates of hell
Negotiate time placation for a cure.

Sunday 29th June 2014
The plan was to try to get into St Giles but this was still
unconfirmed. At least the syringe driver had sorted out the
sickness and the cream for my lips was working. I ache all
over and still cannot stomach anything to eat. I got upset with
Mum and told her if I didn't improve she must just let me go
as I'm too poorly to keep fighting if no alternatives are on
offer.

Monday 30th June 2014
I was woken early from a deep horrible sleep with a sleeping
tablet and changes to my driver by not the nicest of nurses in
the world, who insisted on washing my bottom even though I
was managing fine, just so she could put a new needle in my
leg. I felt completely dazed all day. The ambulance men
brought me over to St Giles with lots of in house attitude.

Once I was in the room I started to cry. I never expected to find myself here, it is a beautiful place but after all it is still a hospice! I saw senior doctors and nurses at around 4pm with Simon and we explained the complete story, well Simon did I was just so tired. Plans were put in place for my medication and to get me off the syringe driver as the week goes on, but honestly it looks like I will be here longer than a couple of days.

Dazed and exhausted we left the NHS
That free regime that cares
But is crippled, worried and worn
In constant fear of patient prosecution.
Skip the day, in avoidance of family retribution
Until it becomes a system of only well meant care
Of rattling tea trolley cures
Suffocated in the thin veneer of low wage sincerity.

Do we deserve more? We tax paying mass
We none voting cynical citizens
That relinquish without question monthly hard earned cash
For treatment when needed
That could amount to death, or lip service trash.

I did not look back as we left that seventh house,
Where we touched the thought and vision
That I had almost lost, but recaptured my wife's soul and
spirit
In the passing of your ordinary day.

Tuesday 1st July onwards to 6th July 2014
While the hospice tried to sort me out, I didn't realise how poorly I have actually felt all the way through. Lou came in the evening and sorted my nails out which was lovely as I was beginning to feel such a mess. It was nice to be just the three of us as I was so tired.

Earlier Tina and Cloe came and all the nurses that know Cloe said she should work here, and I agree, she is a complete natural at it. They bought me lovely gifts and were just quiet to talk to. On Thursday Sue and Paul came with a bottle of bubbly, but I found it all so tiring in between as the physio department had come to talk to me about equipment to help with getting about and walking, great! Debbie and Colin saw me again, Deb got quite upset as I was so ill; when she saw me a week ago so she was glad to see me looking so much better.

Saturday 5th July 2014
Had a lovely Jacuzzi bath with Simon there to help me then Helen, Kev Richard, Hayley, Hannah and Jessica came to see me and Lisa from work popped in with more flowers and cards. They are all so lovely. But I felt really shaky and not myself at all, must rest more, even when the others went off to the pub I just wanted to sleep all the time.

I washed her feet today, like some lost disciple
And in some ways I am,
Clinging to her, every piece of her living cloth
To caress and clutch at her warmth
To hold her flesh, it lives and breathes within my touch
Joint acts of kindness that mean so much.

I bathed her body today
This broken tired object of my still craving desire
Still so intimate to me, each curve and line of her female
form
Is still my love, my only love
Her body is just my lust, her mind, her presence is what I
trust.

I wash her once unfathomable hair, drawn to each
remembered curl
That is and was a moment of our lives together
Now out of reach and fallen from our care,
These invisible strands of DNA
Are lost and blown, poisoned away.

But in time they will return
Roll around my fingers in endless play
In our belief that our former life
Was not for nothing, not to be silently swept away
At the end of a busy working day.

Sunday 7th July 2014

Really bad night, felt sick and just wanted to lie on the floor flat. All night the nurses went beyond the call of duty, they changed the mattress and put it on the floor with pillows and then Lindsey rubbed my back while I was down there. Simon arrived around 4.30am poor thing, finally settled me around 4.50am and I reckon I dropped off to sleep then.

Monday 7th July 2014

Cancelled all visitors as I felt bad. Just stick to seeing Simon, Mum and Norman until I feel a bit stronger. We've had lots of meetings with the Doctors who are sorting out my medication slowly.

So Tracey and I travelled across the desert,
This desert that is dry open cancer
This ever fluctuating dune of suffering
We reach a top and slowly slide effortlessly
To the foot of more unknown orphaned anger.

We journeyed from state care
With all its well meaning "you're going to live, you're going
to die".
Anthems of god bless, to them a number, to them one less.
We arrived at an unknown Shangri-La
An oasis in a tree-lined back water lane
All calm all peaceful, unbelievable, a waterfall of care.

When you have battled the tortoise, and raced against the
hare,
To free a mind from a relentless course,
To find a sanctuary of peace to share
Our safe haven, our little chink of light
In this fear, this dark smudge of night.

Each disarming and natural smile,
Each encouraging word in freedom heard
Heals the broken and wounded body, feeds the worried mind
Until you almost fall, fall in love
With the calm, the knowing charm, that you are now safe.

In this enchanted angel present place, we can rebuild.
You unknowingly, effortlessly disarm our anguish and our
hurt
In every easy conversation, our room was a glow
With happy voices and helpful choices.

Too much trouble is a fragile bubble, that they protect on the
wind.
Will not allow a pin to burst, or a gust to separate
For each and every feather of their settled wings
Breathes life and hope to the dying
And cradle the falling families in soft down
Cascading feathers in sunlight fall.

In memory that we were held safe
Until god takes us, takes us all.
Her life, my wife, my only connection with the sun, sea and
eternity
Our brief stain on the curvature of this earth.

This, my impending ultimate loss
But your ultimate, new line, new life reborn.
Our everyday haunted hope
That the days are long before the days we mourn.

Tuesday 8th July 2014
Poor Mum and Norman broke down on the way home from
St Giles. Fortunately they had telephone numbers on them
(two switched on cookies). Apparently a radiator part had
gone but the guy sorted it really quickly. They were so tired.
Mum had helped me bathe so she was extra tired.

After they had left Simon and I decided to go for a drive, the
sandwiches we had were so dry. I asked Simon if he would
drive me home - what a difference being home on your own
loo, and in your own bed, the garden and kitchen all looked
amazing, but as Simon said, it was a bridge too far really.

It wasn't today I had a bath, it was Monday or Wednesday. I'm so confused.

Wednesday 9th July 2014
Spoke to physio again as I thought they would help me, which to be fair they did. They got me a lovely clean wheel chair and a seat walker thing, all really useful and free of charge.

Jon came to see me on his own which was so wonderful, it was a real delight to see him and as usual he made me laugh. I got him talking to one of the pretty nurses who are all so kind to me. He wheeled me around the gardens and grounds. Saw the pigeons in the trees, and the fishes. Jon helped put me to bed for a rest, I'm knackered again!

Thursday 10th July 2014
Simon and Jon saw doctors about their ailments, both of which Doctor Rees doesn't seem unduly worried about, but if not sorted it will be, on my next appointment. I will help them source outcomes.

Friday 11th July 2014
The doctors all agree that if we can minimise syringe driver then I can go home. I wanted to jump off the ceiling I was so pleased. Everything is going in that direction but I'm still being very careful not to overdo anything.

I was able to leave at around 3.10pm and it was the longest morning ever waiting for all the pills and the schedule on what to take and when. Then finally it was time to leave. We had bought two large boxes of Thornton's chocolates for them all, and there were lots of hugs and kisses. It was a good release I think.

If there are hospital beds with hospital corners,
Are there hospice beds with hospice corners?
Their spirits, tucked safe within the folds, the blankets of the
ill.

If there is the failing money of the National Health
Is there a lighted place, to fight the demons that hinder
recovery?
And if laid bare to die, set free,
Release a life, forgo restraint from god and his religion,
He to count the silver of your memory to one single day.
Clutch the hand of your own personal unknown belief,
Escape this world, and fly, cut loose a life from faith's
indecision.

If there is fear of growing, crippling pain
Is there relief? Is there trust, in ultimate blind eye fall
To rest and bask in slumbers gained.
If the ice in your drink has options as to how it dissolves,
Surly the volunteers form part of the healing,
The encountered spirits of resolve?

If the pinkies clean our room with an easy smile every day,
Surely the pain, that anguish will diminish, fade away?
We had never, and never will again, encounter
A time, a place where peace prevailed,
Where hope in tiny boats with little white sails
Set a course on the streams of dreams.

If the whole mass of life in adjoining rooms
Are able to reach and talk, of impending loss and
bereavement,
It is solely down to this untouchable air of kindness and
security
That is born out of some unique, priceless human courage of
achievement.

Saturday 12th July 2014

Bless her, it's poor Davina's Birthday and she has no card and no gift what so ever. I don't feel happy; she also has a broken hip. Mum came late morning, it was wonderful to see her, they just pottered about and I stayed in bed but we did sit outside briefly. Again, I was quiet. Lou got all funny with mum as she said she hasn't seen much of her. She went out later to work a bar at the Moseley Folk festival, all guns a blazing. Helen then arrived and saw me in bed, she was looking lovely and all made up but I didn't care, she made me laugh. Then she, Simon and Kevan went off to the pub to sort some paperwork out on the sale of Davina's house. I relaxed and had a bath. Another not great night, more aches and pains which would not go. I finally succumbed to the pills to try and sort it out.

Sunday 13th July 2014

I had a fabulous day after a rubbish tummy ache start. Had a long lie in and chilled, we then went for a walk in Newhall Valley. The walk was beautiful, very special, and the weather was great. We had a laugh and also popped to look for garden seats again but still found nothing we like. Then we came home to prepare a family dinner, which was lovely. Simon seems to love cooking now, everything he touches is scrummy. Jon and I were very impressed with dinner tonight, it was all gorgeous and Jon helped by clearing it all away, he then disappeared to watch the World Cup, but we did have a laugh over dinner and how we should be putting Simon on Facebook. Not a good idea I am sure, alternative ego!

Lying in bed hoping not to get tummy pain but can't really pre-empt it, so just enjoying my special evening, waiting for ideas of what to wear tomorrow not sure what for though. Never mind, it will come to me.

Monday 14th July 2014

New day, everyone was off to work except for Simon, who was up like a lark. The man came to do the bushes, he did a really tidy job and finally convinced Simon, and he agrees, that the job is a good-un. I had a good rest of the day in the garden in a bit of sun. The weather was good; Mum says I should take some honey extract, which I am happy to. We had a laugh over some cakes, and later Simon rode me in the wheelchair to the Jamboree stone in the park. Watched a programme about training school for the paras. It was a good day.

I am having to write my journal in the middle of the night as I can't sleep, cannot get this one to three o'clock barrier out of my head. I'm not sure why I can't sleep. So I went downstairs but it was horribly dark and chilly and there was nothing on TV. How do people survive? I wonder if Tina is awake now or not?

Tuesday 15th July 2014

Awake early again, the pain seems to start before 8am but with tablets, a hot water bottle and usual oramorph, it starts to subside. I'm extremely tired, all in the bottom of my back and legs. Had eggs for breakfast and mushroom soup for lunch, oh delight. Simon took me out in the car to Next, Boots and M&S. There was nothing to buy at all but I felt brighter when we got back home. The nutritionist rang from St Giles; she said I need protein and very rich creamy food to build me back up. Simon did the most amazing tea again tonight, salmon with pesto, sun-dried tomatoes, honey, creme fraiche, watercress and soya beans with salad and new potatoes. If nothing else, this could become one really brilliant cancer cook book haha! He prepared mine early and I ate nearly all of it, which was possibly not a good idea as later on I went downhill. I started to feel claustrophobic again like last night, and a bit sick. Simon made up the spare bed just in case, which is a good idea, and Lou took me up to bed. I started to feel very queasy, hot and sick the minute they closed the window, then surely, like some slow moving tide, the sickness just welled up. Fortunately it was only once but I did feel crappy.

Jon and Si rubbed my tummy this time until it subsided, and then Si slept in the fourth bedroom, which would have been fine until I had a wasp come in the room. I finally had to ask him to get rid of it as Lou and Jon were asleep, although I had pranced around after it for quite a while myself first. I did let him back into our bed afterwards.

Wednesday 16th July 2014

We collected Mum and Norman from their house to go and find me some new underwear from M&S in Tamworth. We had a real laugh and spent ages in there. There was no underwear but found a great pair of trousers and a couple of tops which I am very pleased with. Getting used to using the wheelchair, it's all really comfy and a lot of fun. Afterwards, we needed some food so set off for the Crown at Elford. Mum and I used to come here for a treat, but it was closed so we ended up at a pub in Wiggington, near Sarah and Richard's, which was fine. We had baguettes, and all round it was really relaxed and fun. Dropped them off home and headed back for a sleep.

Thursday 17th July 2014

The physio from St Giles came at 9.30am. It was all interesting stuff, then Paul bought us round a fan to use which was great. Little Liz who I used to work with came to see me, she does seem to get a bit upset but enjoys coming I think, and we have set another date.

Went off to Pershore for a walk/push by the river and to see the church and town. We had nice chicken tikka sandwiches in a cafe, which would have been nicer on white bread I have decided. So warm sitting by the river and being in the sun. Poor Simon, his Mum has got to go into a home as her dementia is getting worse. How many plans we all have that never come to fruition, that have to be altered before they are put in to creation. Shit, shit, shit.

Saw Dr Anwar on my own as Simon was trying to park the car. It was fine really; they just say it how it is, as the cancer is extensive. The drain worked well and there was no fluid at present. I was offered no alternatives for fatigue, or how not to feel tired so much as it is all down to the cancer, and that was the problem. The plan is for Simon to speak to the London Hospital about this trial and to get this up and running again as soon as possible.

Friday 18th July 2014
Two calls made to London about the trial, but to no avail. Simon will keep trying.

We went to Sue and Paul's Friday night and had a fab time. We had a great welcome and felt comfortable. We were all relaxed and had a laugh. I do feel like impending doom though as everyone knows that I am on limited time, which is strange and a bit bizarre. Mandy asked me what I was scared of. I said it was not being asleep. I just want to be out of it quite early on and not be waiting for each bit to happen and for it not to be long and drawn out. I think Nigel keeps getting upset as he knows the inevitable, but I'm not sure even I have come to terms with the inevitable.

Turn a month and see within,
See all unravel, in lives that have been
Like children not taking the medicine of truth.
Our brutal meetings with well meaning medics,
With their screens of binary truth,
These slaves to nought and one
But between the codes, a grasp is lost, I will not bare it when
it's gone.

A simple human impulse for comfort of hanging on,
It lasts it shines through time,
That time that was yours and mine,
Our clouds and our sunshine,
Your stars, your moon, your dawn and dusk.
I am now blown corn, an empty husk.

Bury me deep under the earth, silent cold and still
For if I live I will feed on the ill.
For we will not be skipping around the lake of love;
I have jumped in, prepared to drown. With the ripples of our
life
I swallow the memories, so I cannot breathe.
Sink, let me sink to the bottom of life
Never to exhale, only inhale and hold our love.

To drown in breathless memory,
Fragments of truth within the water,
Separated, the currents pulling, 'til we are parted.
For what we started, for what we believed in,
For that thin gasp of air was, our lives
Suffocated now and stifled, but held deep within.

Saturday 19th July 2014

Took some sleeping pills last night and although I slept okay I have felt really down all day, miserable and low. All I can see is the end. I have complete lethargy, no energy, feel down and don't know what to say to the family. Simon cooked a fabulous lunch again; fish, peas and mash. It looked and tasted amazing; I'm certainly getting my appetite back.

Sent him off to see Angela and Matt, I didn't feel up to it at all. It's not a good day for socialising for me today, which is really sad because I love Ang and Matt. But Simon went off to see them, I did text them as felt awful as I had had a nice time on Friday with others, and the pictures were on Facebook.

Felt so grim mood wise all day Saturday. It was a crappy day, I over-ate I think, to build me up, but it just makes me feel worse. I will look at this again with Simon, but his food is delicious.

Simon was pretty much at the end of his tether when I went to bed, said he couldn't cope with it all. It doesn't help when the kids are getting ready to go out, and our lives are so fucked!

The footsteps of a nightmare hasten towards my door,
Their drum roll grows, its din blinds my mind and thought,
Makes my hairs stand cold, my body sweat and twist
In its ever thickening blinding mist.

Vibrating thoughts, little circles of life
Captured within electrical circuits that jump and pulse,
Trying to find a seconds worth of freedom in hovering open
air,
To live just one night, one day, without a single care.

But still I hear the candour of heavy boots,
Searching out, seeking out our door, our pain
Offering a communion for the amnesia of our lives
In exchange for the miasma of our dreams.
Our lives have become insignificant,
Our lives have become deficient.
If the life's work of a bee is a glorious third of a teaspoon of
honey,
Then why are we not all satisfied with that small spoon of
sticky happiness,
Enjoying what we have, cast away the money?

Tonight I struggled and in guilt I failed.
Confused, I walked away, so did part of our love also slip,
Lost in the paths of your pains,
The start of the dying away.

My head held in my hands,
I gathered my sorrowful mind
And walked the stair to your door
To recapture the kindness that I had let slip
The needing eye of us both, that was lost
In the crossfire of care.

This the closest thing we can muster to a disagreement
That is fuelled, fired then calmed
By our knowing, haunting close bereavement.
Troubled by my own mind
To love but also to resent this love
That I now struggle to sometimes understand.

I do not want to let her go,
But her eyes are full of other skies, not this planet's ties.
For peace to rest away from her cruel, growing liaison,
This broken body that never allows her sleep
And me standing useless
Against her now worn, smooth planed heart.

Am I letting her go, this fight that now meets soft
submission?
Are my eyes meeting her new horizons,
Allowing a loved one to leave and look beyond
From my life and her chastened awakening?
Can I save her, can I cut her loose?
Will I allow a love so strong to pass
Her chance to join with freedom?

Sunday 20th July 2014

Finally must have slept Saturday night, but it seemed so disjointed and I can't get certain thoughts out of my head. Today we went off to Walmley for a walk/ride in the wheelchair. It does me good every time. I'm so weary but this seems to inject me with energy every time really, I love going.

When finished, we went to Asda for a couple of bras and then picked some poppies which I have dried to keep for my memory box. I need to go to Boots to sort out the photos for the same box. Came home grabbed soup and then Louise, James and Auntie Mel came. It was a great afternoon, warm and sunny. Mel does come out with some wonders, she said to Simon, "have you thought about praying to Saint Jude, the saint of hope and impossible causes?" as I'm so far gone!
Anyway, lovely chicken dinner later from Mum, I added a spring cabbage, it was very tasty. I made a rhubarb crumble and sorted out the fridge as it keeps leaking and then freezing up, which is a real pain. Hopefully it is sorted now.

Got uncomfortable as the night went on, sitting on each and every chair in the lounge trying to get comfy. It all just gets to me eventually, I wonder if the hospice supply beds in the end?

I did try some ibuprofen this morning which seemed to work, I'm not sure it was okay though. But Viv said it was and it felt like an alternative pain killer, so I don't carer really. Off to buy garden chairs tomorrow if we can.

Monday 21st July 2014

I did sleep okay but had that horrid shaky feeling again. But it didn't get too bad. I took a while to feel okay in the morning, not so shaky now but hey ho.

Set off to the Range and found a great chair for £60, it sort of matches the others and has an infinity recliner on it so can catch the sun while lying flat, which is great. I did almost get stuck in one of the other low recliners though and had to get Simon to get me out of it, which was really scary. It's the lack of strength in the back of your legs that gives way. I understand what Norman means now on the subject, I wouldn't like to be on my own in a department store, or anywhere else for that matter.

So we got a chair, but couldn't get cushions for the swing seat. I'm not sure we ever will get proper ones; I don't want to pay loads. We still tried B&Q and Homebase but gave up and came home. Rested in my new very relaxing chair with Simon and Jon for a bit. I do think I need to keep having restingfull (?) days - good word haha! The afternoon and evening was all good, Lou painted my nails red for me. We did have more wasps in the bedroom later - will have to sort that tomorrow.

Tuesday 22nd July 2014

Rested in a little but as it was such beautiful weather we collected Mum and Norman and went to New Hall Valley for a walk. Jon came too and everyone pushed my chair. A lot of people including Mum's neighbours keep saying how well I look. I hope I do, I would hate to look well and be going massively downhill.

After the knackering walk, poor Mum had hurt her back and toe from a fall the other day, so we went for a drink at the Jockey then dropped them home and me home for a big rest.

Had M&S stew which was tasty, am having to get used to resting loads more. We have arranged for Debbie and Angela to pop in after 4pm. I'm quite excited just got to freshen up and get dressed again after my lie down, pheeeww!

It was nice to see Debs and Angela, they all tucked into a G&T while I sucked on my orange juice, but no problem. I love my new garden chair especially as the sun was out.

Fab tea again, I only had a small piece of salmon but I think it was still too much again. Need still smaller amounts. I washed it down with tablets and milk but my stomach got upset again! I want to sleep with the lights off, but I'm scared to turn the lights off. I just cannot drop off writing notes again, this is such a pain. Roll on morning.

Wednesday 23rd July 2014 - 8st 5lb

Jenny, Norman's daughter, is over from Oz for a bit to see us all. I have got my pillow under my legs which feels good. I can rest this morning. Waited ages for Jenny to arrive as she had lost her car keys on the house boat she was staying in owned by her mother in law. When she arrived she was so warm and friendly.

Just wanted to say how lovely it is when Jon sees me on the landing and comments on how pretty I look, whether I have just got up or walking out of the shower he mentions my appearance. It's such a boost when you feel like shit.

Anyway, as expected Jenny was warm and friendly and did not stop talking the whole of the time she was with us. She's a lovely lady and She's very into her healing, her horses and dogs and what she can do with it, quite rightly. She did say to Simon that she wanted to see me again while she was over here and hadn't got loads of plans. But we will have to see how all this pans out really.

They left about 3ish for me to have a rest, which I dutifully did all afternoon. Simon went into see them all at work and I slept probably on and off all afternoon and into the evening. I still wish I had some spare energy, they all say it is natural but just wish I could pick up a bit more.

In the evening Simon watched the opening ceremony for the Commonwealth Games and I dozed in bed to all the channel four food programmes. Great!

Thursday 24th July 2014

Sarah was coming to see us; she's a lovely lady and such a great friend, always knows what to say. Just beforehand Polly Waites arrived laden with rose plants which was a lovely thought. She is so bright, fresh and alive, off to go canoeing in Stratford. It was just such a kind thought to drop off these Roses.

When Polly left, Sarah promptly arrived and we sat in the garden. It was a beautiful day again, Sarah looking all fresh and clean in her Wedgewood dress. I just wish I had more energy to really enjoy all of my friends. I am now 8st 3lb. Must try and gain some weight from these meals but if I eat too much, it makes me sick.

The good thing is that the swelling in my ankle has gone, and the pins and needles in my leg has also gone. I wish someone was keeping a better eye on my blood levels to see how I am doing.

Anyway, felt really tired while Sarah was here so had to go to bed early which was fine as she chatted with Simon. I dropped off for a bit then when we had grabbed some food we went to the park for a wheelchair push as Simon now calls it. It's wonderful weather, I can't believe Simon has never been able to enjoy this time as he was always at work 9 to 5.

You try it.
These days of confusion, of broken fusion inside my head,
Fire crackers break and burst my thoughts,
An instant glow, but a lost spark a fading ember,
Remembered in our laughter, the brightest flash and flame
Before the tallow dies, and is gutted to this world.

You try it.
Watch the courage of the dying, being governed by a matter
of time,
Counselled and stretched by the living,
My every wakening moment, leaves the sweat and strain of a
former life
To feaster and turn on my sunken pillow.

You try it, if you can,
Not to understand how a day will end,
Not to comprehend how far love will stretch,
To recapture, keep a peaceful end, an end to our day.

You try it.
Loving what is now slipping away, being blown away,
Try lying with the former comet, burning bright in your bed
Dragging you within her fiery tail, into another morn.

You try it.
Push your wife for a walk
With condescending looks from strangers, that suddenly
want to talk
Their freedom to walk on by,
To never hear the families crying nightly lullaby.

You try it, if you can,
Have a life governed by the parade of pills,
Constant time check to ensure continued pain relief,
A draining timetable for us both
A stealing of our lives by the latch key thief.

Go on, you brave heart.
Wipe a slate clean with anger, grow old and jealous for what
might have been,
What plans we could have weaved across this world,
What threads we could have laid for children yet to come,
But now our memory will be lost in a tapestry of regret,
Our children will carry a darkened heart
That will sit within the undertow of every future happy event.

You try it,
You heavy full confident soul, try running on empty
For the sake of the one that is all to you.
You blissful being under your lazy dawn,
Full of retirements affordable, comfortable angst.
Don't worry I will not burst your bubble, stain your sight
Or steal your rose tinted view, for you made it, you saw it
through.
Happy to talk to us for a while,
But don't try it, don't walk our daily mile.

After the walk we went to M&S for some ready meals but it was so cold in there, we picked what I wanted and came home for a rest. Si went back to Tesco, poor bloke, he must be knackered. Then we just chilled in the conservatory in to the evening, Simon cleaned all my nails off which felt better so I might leave them for a bit.

Slept on my own in the big bed again. Was loads better, but can Simon seriously sustain this? He will have to buy a proper bed really. I don't think I actually slept properly, but have dozed loads better.

Friday 25th July 2014
Got up early to see Viv from the hospice who was on time. I tried to explain how terribly tired I feel constantly, she did mention about speaking to Neil at the hospice for me, to see if he could help. I will ring her on Monday.

After all this I rested briefly, then went to buy more food to top up my calorie intake. Later on in the afternoon, and after a lot of sleeping, I woke up feeling terrible, sweaty, shaky and with no energy. It felt like my blood sugars were low.

I rang the doctors and saw Dr Clarke, who was amazing thank goodness. She took all my bloods, and told me I looked okay, and put me on anti depressants. God willing something will help me feel less jittery soon, that would help. I slept quite well, poor Simon was on the floor again but think he is going to buy a Z bed.

Saturday 26th July 2014

Jenny bought loads of beautiful food over as a gift for us, Mum and Norman were really kind, but sadly I feel too poorly to spend time with them all. I just want to get to Monday (London).

We had a trip out to again to buy more food, went to Pype Hayes Park with its wheelchair access. It was not fab but we did a little walk. I still feel everything has been sucked out of me, a good night's sleep I think!

Sunday 27th July 2014

Stayed in bed most of the day, Mum popped round which was a bit of a highlight, she was in good spirits and cheered Simon, Jon and I up. Norman was very sweet too, just kind and caring, the way he stroked my hand gently.

Spent all day except lunch time in bed, which Simon says will heal me, so I am doing as I am told. I hope I sleep okay tonight.

Lovely to have my children in bed with me, Lou is going to do my nails again. She has an enormous bruise from falling over on Saturday; Jon plucked my chin for me. It's funny how we are all at a resigned state of mind.

My daughter has gone to bed early, filled with storms of
dread.
My son walks abroad distorted thoughts inside his head.
Each compartment of their grief
Is held so carefully between what is past, and what is yet to
come.

They have known the Calvary mother
The crucifix love of self denial for another,
She accepts this disease like iron through her wrists
She was born to see and touch the love of self created eyes,
I was born to marvel at unconditional ties.

When all is said and done
Our children will have cried, broken, realising that the race is
run.
I will have kneeled, weak, marvelling at the stars,
Her stars, beyond our fetid sullen skies.

We remaining three shall separate truth from lies,
We will in a hollow sense live lives
And I their orbit, their gravity be,
Their reminder that hope was buried in cruel travesty.
It is her legacy, her light, her majesty.

If there is to be a voyage around a father,
Let me pull in all,
The lost, the good, that heated desire.
The need to remember the low fire,
The passing days of love,
The summer air, the need and want, of life's journey on this
one way street.
The sound of wedding bells and little hands and feet.

Virgin skies to start and try again,
Generations of love and emotion
For life is but a drug, an addiction,
An endless stream, a chain, a glorious notion.

Monday 28th July 2014

Woke up early after sleeping really well and was ready to go to London, so didn't feel too bad. Filled back of the car with loads of pillows and I lay in the back and slept most of the way. It was a tiny clinic and not easy to see what the hell was happening; nurses, consultants and registrars everywhere.

Finally saw the consultant who was a delight, but did not think I had the energy for the trial and said he would write back to Dr Anwar etc, to see if my meds could be altered slightly. That evening Dr Clark called to say my white blood cells had twice been high, and will put me on some antibiotics to clear the infection. I was happy to agree.

Feel strangely enlightened this evening not just tired, I do have a bit of hope. Felt sick earlier so am taking it really easy to see if it passes, hope to sleep well, can't cope with not sleeping. The kiddies came and sat on the bed with me again for a while which was lovely.

Tuesday 29th July 2014

Had a long lie in as Sue and Steve were coming at 1pm. It was lovely to see them although I keep getting upset as we all know what is coming and it makes me and everyone I see sad. After they went we ate and then set off for Costco, where we attached a trolley to the front of my wheelchair, oh the joys of my life now. Scooted round for quite a while with Simon, he was happy to be in charge of what we were looking at and buying, and so was I. We did have a laugh as he ended up pushing me and a trolley loaded with catering sized washing powder and meat packs etc. Back home I helped him tidy the food away a bit and then lay in the conservatory for the remainder of the evening. The air and the light was perfect, it wasn't too hot for a change and especially with Sarah's bunting she bought us blowing determinedly in the wind. I hope it doesn't break too soon as it is so pretty, like those prayer flags in Nepal or wherever they are.

Off to bed now, writing my journal quite late. Had a good cry with Simon reading his lovely poems, so glad I have someone like him to take care of me.

Pay one hundred percent attention to me, she said.
As if I wouldn't,
Because I know that this time has a consequence.
I will remember her love, her smell, her essence
As it will be lost to me
And the silence will be the noise, the rattle in my head.

Of lists long written of holidays and hopes,
Thrust and crushed within this shortened future.
A lifetime in a spark, so vibrant, so painfully dark.
I am now fearful of each new day.
The sun and its glow, that globe with its fiery talons
Will kiss the cold curtains of our room,
We awake and die within its dawn
We talk of life, we talk of death,
We talk and lie about heaven's breath.

Her weakness of spirit against another day
Is my burden to absorb, to love her even more and take it
away,
For she is my spreading fire, my virgin desire
We know now this world, this life
Has set a compass, its finger
A diseased touch, at she, my family and me.

The decay of a body with such incandescent eyes is hard to
comprehend.
I have walked, followed and basked
In every mysterious layer of her eye
But the dark pupil is the centre of her, of every woman that
you want to know
And when you see it you have it, you live for its gaze, its
glow.

But now I slowly have to release
Those eyes held full of truth
That will fade and close to me
Left with a life, a life in which to die
To recall our remembrance dance, a shopping day glance
Now such a distant intense face of burning love.

Wednesday 30th July 2014

A late start, really jittery. Simon went off to Tesco and mum came round. My clothes are all really big for me now. We are all a bit low, no great shakes anymore to make the outcome any different so finding it hard to lift ourselves up.

Went to bed at about 3pm, Mum tried to tell me to pray, "you have got to believe". Everyone is praying so hard for me she said. She is so inspirational and strong at times. At 5pm Simon went off to see Dave which was really good for him, I'm glad he went. Dave obviously wants to make friends with Steve, so there's some leg work still to be done there.

After a while I made the effort to come downstairs and sit with Lou and then Simon while they ate. My food was good today, macaroni cheese with extra cheese and croutons made from toast, then scallops, potatoes, tomatoes and mushrooms along with asparagus, then later still a steamed pudding along with a solero, and I picked at a packet of peanuts. Got to be lots of calories surely, just need to turn it into energy PLEASE. Off to bed at 10ish feeling relaxed.

Thursday 31st July 2014

Rested in bed in the morning then had a nice shower and got dressed and made up a bit to see Jenny. They hadn't eaten and arrived early but it didn't really matter. I felt bright and cheery, and Mum was happy to see me looking brighter. We had a good time. After a while they left to have lunch and I rested. Later on I came down and watched TV with Simon.

Friday 1st August 2014

Not a great day woke up feeling low. Saw Viv but it was all a bit flat, I had tummy pain which kept on niggling all day. I wondered if it was because we had reduced the patch on my arm, Viv suggested I saw the Doctor so we went in the afternoon. Doctor Rees confirmed the need to increase the patch back up, and suggested that was probably why I was in pain. He also said to get Vanessa the Macmillan nurse to organise a scan to see if the fluid is returning in my tummy.

Saturday 2nd August 2014

Jenny rang early and asked if she could pop over as she was at a loose end which was fine as we had nothing specific to do. Chatted about nothing in particular but she is just so lovely to me and wants to do so much but obviously it is all about the counselling than being able to actually do anything. She also gave me the chemical symbol in a silver necklace for the anti-depressant I am taking. She has the matching earrings so it is like a link between us.

The rest of the day was quite good and I stayed up with Simon, had a mouthful of red wine and a curry starter which was lovely.

Sunday 3rd August 2014

Tina came with Cloe at 10.30am to see me, they gave me a good pep talk and bought me a lovely Orchid, pyjamas and chocolate; such wonderful thoughtful girls. Cloe spoke to Simon about my tablets too, suggesting a couple that might be making me more tired if taken twice a day, so I will speak to Viv about that. Rang Mum to ask her to come a bit earlier to see me, she was pleased I looked so well and I did make an effort not to get upset again today with her, as I know it hurts her.

Simon cooked me a lovely meal and we sat in the conservatory while I ate it. Sat outside when it was warm enough, chatted briefly about the funeral again as think Mum wants to talk to him about costs etc.

Later on I had a bath while Jon and Si had dinner together, just in bed now writing my journal, feeling weary.

SILENCE NOW

C S Lewis wrote, if you want the love you have to have the pain. That's the deal.

Friday 8th August 2014

We awoke to another day, a day filled with a certain amount of hope hanging nervously in the air, maybe today would see a change, her pain controlled and we begin a glorious fight back, energy slowly restored, yes with another drug, but just to have that chance to see her once more leading the hours that form a day, planning the weeks that held our lives together.

The consultant was coming from St Giles to re-evaluate her pills, her pain and her lethargy, as her current pill intake was not cutting the mustard.

My camp bed faced the opposite way to our double bed so as I had done for the last four weeks I woke and looked across the void that now separated us, all the love and hurt that lay in that small two foot gap, was sometimes too much for us both to bare, but the space and single comfort of that double bed was what she needed.

So, as I said I looked across the void, her eyes met mine, a smile, a thumbs up meant we were okay today. I took Lou to the station in my gym jams as I always do, returned, made coffee and got back into our bed. I lay beside her and we talked.

Steel and stone
You lay my heart upon your throne
And effortlessly cut me to the bone.
Your eyes are my strength
What am I supposed to do when they close, close for the last
time?
And her soul is lost to me,
Given to the heavens for eternity.

I am left weak, on your memory
Futile visits to a cemetery
Trying to understand, reconcile our lives, and its lost
symmetry.

We both held our hands upward toward the sun
But life cast our palms to the earth,
The decaying of our lives
Left us crying in the ultimate garden
Of all that we had and all that I let slip so quietly through my
fingers.

To dream that belief again,
Fresh and new in a tight held fist.
I will always blame my grasp for your distance
Your technicolor life, my insignificance.
I held beauty
I held truth
I held life
And oh I loved the strife
I want to bleed, cut deep by her knife
The only true and real pain.

If you find one true love and then witness its passing,
You will close your heart
You will privately fall apart
You will turn your heel and catch that country cart
Lay down with meadow flowers
Fragrance rich in a smile so lost
My remaining years will be my bill of sale, my cost.

Forever recalling her encapsulating charm
That life, that warmth, I crave every day,
The day you went away.

The pains in her tummy were returning as they sometimes did in the morning so I was not alarmed. I think I rubbed her back, her tummy and her sides as that normally did the trick. But these pains didn't want to leave; they grew and began to twist her inside. I noticed her skin so soft, so complete, was slightly colder and clammy to my touch. No matter, the Doctor from St Giles is coming at 10.30am and it is now 8.30am so not long to go.

We shuffled across the landing to the bathroom as she was uncomfortable, all over more nervous than ever before, more unsettled. I was not aware that these would be our last moments, how could I? But I carry a measure of guilt with me each day that weighs against each smile that I conjure from the depths of suffering and loneliness.

The vomit that left her and spattered on the bathroom floor, was it her anger, was it her final act of defiance to get this fucking thing out of her? Or just a last nail of indignation against her glory.

I spent time trying to tidy up as it was just sick, I have seen more of it in the last three months than you will ever see, but I look back now and think I should have left it to stain the floor with its acid, its remnants of a life.

We struggled back to the bedroom after Jon had lent over and kissed her goodbye before he went to work, as she lay broken on the cold tiled bathroom floor.

She sat on the bed all muddled, desperate and confused. "Touch my head, hold my arms", she said. And then it happened, her head fell back and a gasp of life left her.

You cannot imagine the panic, the sheer desperation, the futility of being human as the woman of your complete existence starts to dissolve and vanish.

How shall I carry the dead yet again,
Stones in my pocket, turned by weary fingers
Held within tired empty hands?
So much family loss cannot be easily reconciled;
My father, my brother, my wife, she my lover
Are scattered silent on the water
No returning voices are ever heard upon the waves of death,
But still we turn and stare in busy streets
In hopeful anticipation of their former breath.

Do I succumb to a certain acceptance of this life and its pain?
Let the glowing part of me drown in wanton grief,
Selfish in helpless arrival of the letting go
To embrace and love the loss, the irreversible flow?

The sirens rang in my ears as I pumped her chest in selfish needing to hold on to what little life she had left, the gasping and the fight pulling between what lay ahead and what fell behind were our last loving moments on God's cruel Earth.

So what have I learnt against what I have lost? Possibly everything, but maybe nothing, all that comes to mind is a poem, written in the Shakespeare pub in town, when our days were filled with nothing but happiness and kisses. It came from Tracey and her ability to love each day.

Venture forth beyond your cloud
Throw off your sorrowful shroud
Look at your life as a sunrise, stare at its wonder and be proud
You have managed your demons. You have talked with them, sat with them,
Invited them to join your noise, your madding crowd.
Could you say that you finally accept your fleeting chance for a rainbows end?
It is your life to spend,
Not a duty to any fractured family to defend.

Your life is a dawn and a single sunset
With as much misery or joy that you want to give or receive in between,
So let life be your friend, sit with it on a sofa
Take it for a stroll
Teach it to look not at a part but at the whole.

For the blink of an eye will not remember what went before,
Only what comes into view
And a landscape of a life is made by a precious few,
The stars anticipate your own dawn
The brightness only measured by how you raise your head from a pillow's morn.

Click the heels of your favourite shoes
And spark out to another day
You are your own ray of sunlight, held within life's alibi
Allow your mind to fly, free as flowing water
Be as curious as a clergyman's daughter
Running over stones, not raking over the old broken bones.

Your spirit caught up in the spray
Those droplets of you fall, effortlessly away
To join the flow of life and tide,
With all your loved ones held close by your side.

Good night to you.

9852261R00101

Printed in Great Britain
by Amazon.co.uk, Ltd.,
Marston Gate.